PRAYING *from the* HEART

True Stories *of*
Extraordinary Answers
to Prayer

PRAYING *from the* HEART

Edited by *James Stuart Bell*

New York, New York

Acknowledgments
All material that originally appeared in Guideposts publications is reprinted with permission. Copyright © Guideposts. All rights reserved.

Scripture quotations are taken from the *Holy Bible, New Living Translation,* copyright 1996. Used by permission of Tyndale House Publishers, Inc., Wheaton, Illinois 60189. All rights reserved.

Editorial, research, and content development managed by Whitestone Communications, with the assistance of Jeanette Gardner Littleton, Publication Services.

www.guideposts.com
(800) 932-2145
Guideposts Books & Inspirational Media

Cover design by Brand Navigation
Interior design by Gretchen Schuler-Dandridge

Printed and bound in the United States of America
10 9 8 7 6 5 4 3

CONTENTS

INTRODUCTION

"Call to me and I will answer you and show you great and unsearchable things . . . . "

The promise in Jeremiah 33:3 was made thousands of years ago, but it still holds true in our lives today. The God who led the Israelites to victory is still at work, producing victory, meeting needs, answering prayers.

Whether our prayers are as small and intangible as a silent heartfelt desire, or as vast and concrete as an exploding oilrig, God listens. God hears. God answers.

In the pages of this book, you'll find the stories of people who've seen, heard, and felt such answers. Some turned to God immediately; some called on Him as a last resort. But as they called from the depth of their hearts, God heard. And God acted. Often more creatively or powerfully than they asked or even thought. And He can do the same for you.

God delights in meeting our needs, calming our hearts, showing us His love. He is always available to listen to anything we want to communicate–from the whispers of our souls to our impassioned, desperate pleas.

As you read through these pages, may they inspire you and renew your faith that the God of the whole universe hears your whispers and cares about your life.

Come, experience the hope of the Lord and the incredible, invincible power of prayer.

the PRAYER CONVOY *on* I-70

Ron Lantz

Traffic on I-70 wasn't too bad. I should have been enjoying myself on that October day, sitting in the cab of my 18-wheeler, cruising through the Pennsylvania hills.

Thirty-six years as a trucker, and I still got a kick out of my rig. Bass Transportation bought this six hundred-horsepower tractor in 2000. I was the only one who drove it, and although I'd logged almost forty thousand miles, the cab was still so clean you could eat off the floor. If the traffic held steady, I would make my usual run right on schedule, hauling a tanker of building compound from Ohio to Delaware, then deadheading back to my home in Ludlow, Kentucky.

But I didn't make the run on time that day for the same reason I wasn't enjoying the trip.

The Beltway sniper.

The words hammered in my head. Eight dead and two wounded already at the hands of this anonymous assassin, and it didn't look like there'd be an end to it. At any truck stop in the Washington, DC, area, all truckers talked about was the white van the police were looking for. Schools were closed, people too scared to leave their homes.

It weighed on me that this guy was out there getting ready to kill again. I knew what it was like to lose someone you love. Five years earlier my wife, Ruth, and I had lost our son, Ron, to multiple sclerosis.

The day he died had been a pretty October day, just like this one. I knew when I got to the nursing home that something was up because a lot of hollering filled the hall.

"What's going on?" I asked.

"It's your son, Mr. Lantz," a nurse said.

I hurried to Ron's room. Our boy sat on the edge of his bed, hands raised over his head, praising the Lord. For more than a year he hadn't been able to sit up on his own.

"I'm leaving here," Ron said. "Someone's coming through that door tonight to take me home." Then he looked at me real hard. "Dad, I don't want to be up in heaven waiting for you and find out you don't make it."

It wasn't the first time he'd brought up the subject. Ron was a real committed Christian. My parents raised me in the faith, but somehow I'd drifted away.

"I want you to go over to my church right now," Ron went on. "Find my pastor and give your life to the Lord."

Well, that's exactly what I did. Afterward I went back to the nursing home and told Ron. I'm glad I had the chance, because Somebody did come for my boy that night to take him home.

My life turned around. I got active in church. I headed the men's fellowship, led retreats, was on the Sunday school board. I'd never start a run without kneeling by my bed at the rear of the cab and asking God to watch over Ruth. After the sniper shot his first victims, I was praying about that, too, that someone would stop this killing spree. It had lasted for 12 days already.

Around 7:00 PM, when I was about an hour and a half out of Wilmington, Delaware, the usual report came on the radio. Nothing new on the sniper. All they knew was that a white van might be involved.

I started thinking about something I'd learned at church—how a bunch of people praying together can be more powerful than a person praying alone. *What if I get on my CB to see if any drivers want to pull off the road and pray with me about this?*

I pressed the button on my microphone and said that if people wanted to pray about the sniper, they could meet me in half an hour at the eastbound 66-mile-marker rest area. A trucker answered right away. Then another and another. They'd be there. I hadn't gone five miles before a line of trucks formed, some coming up from behind, others up ahead slowing down to join us. The line stretched for miles.

Darkness was falling when I pulled into the rest area filled with at least fifty rigs. In minutes truckers had climbed out of their cabs and sixty or seventy of us, including some wives and children, stood holding hands.

"Let's pray," I said. "Anyone who feels like it can start." Well, the first one to speak up was a kid, maybe ten years old, standing just to my left. The boy bowed his head and started: "Our Father, who art in heaven. . . ."

We went around the circle, some folks using their own words, others using phrases from the Lord's Prayer. I felt there was a special meaning in the phrase, "Deliver us from evil."

The last person finished. We had prayed for 59 minutes. All those truckers adding an hour to their busy schedules!

Ten days later, October 23, I was making my Ohio to Delaware run again. The sniper had struck again.

Right from the start something was different about my trip. In the first place, it was a Wednesday. I normally made my runs Tuesdays and Thursdays. But there was a delay at the loading dock so I told my pastor I'd have to miss our Wednesday night prayer meeting. "We'll pray for you," he said.

The second thing that happened: I was stopped by the police. Once was rare for me. This trip I was pulled over three times. Not for very long, they were just checking papers, but it made me late getting into Wilmington.

The next strange thing: Instead of catching a few hours of sleep, I headed back west as soon as my cargo was offloaded around 11:00 PM. That wasn't like me. I knew too many sad stories of drivers who didn't get enough sleep. It was as if I had an appointment; I couldn't sleep even if I tried.

At midnight the Truckin Bozo show came on the air, a music and call-in program a lot of truckers listen to. The deejays had news in the sniper case. There were two snipers, not one, and officials now believed the guys were driving a blue 1990 Chevrolet Caprice with New Jersey plates, license number NDA–21Z instead of the white van we had been looking for.

I wrote down the tag number. Just before 1:00 AM, I reached the rest stop at the 39-mile-marker near Myersville, Maryland, only a few miles from where so many of us had made a circle and prayed. Westbound on I–70, this was the only rest area with a men's room between Baltimore and Breezewood. I wasn't going to pass that! And the last weird thing about that trip: The truck aisles were full. I'd never seen so many rigs at that stop with drivers asleep. I had to swing around to the car section. I wouldn't be long. Climbing down from my cab, I noticed a car in the No Parking zone. The light over the men's room door was shining right on it.

A blue Chevrolet Caprice.

I looked closer: two men, one slumped over the wheel, asleep. I crept behind some bushes and squinted to make out the license number. Jersey plates: NDA–21Z.

Quiet as I could, I climbed back in my rig.

Better not use the CB in case those guys have one.

I punched 911 on my cell phone. "I'm at the Myersville rest stop. There's a blue Chevrolet Caprice here, New Jersey license number NDA–21Z."

The operator asked me to hold. In a minute she came back with instructions: "Wait there. Don't let them see you. Block the exit with your truck if you can."

If an 18-wheeler can tiptoe, that's what mine did. I blocked as much of the exit ramp as I could, but there was still room for a car to get by. Five minutes passed. Only one other driver was ready to roll. When I told him what was happening, he pulled his rig beside mine, sealing off the exit. I sat in my cab, looking out the side mirrors at that blue Caprice, expecting a shootout and thinking I should be scared. I wondered why I wasn't.

Five more minutes passed. I was afraid another truck or a car would drive up and honk for us to move, waking the suspects, but no one stirred. The cops slid up so quietly I didn't know they were there until suddenly the whole area looked like the Fourth of July with flash-grenades lighting up the night sky to stun the two men.

FBI agents, state troopers, and officers from the sheriff's department swarmed the rest stop. Searchlights. Breaking glass. Shouts. The thump of helicopters, SWAT teams in night-vision goggles, running low, crouching, guns drawn.

Next thing I knew the two men were being led away. The police took names and addresses of everyone who had been at the rest area. Nearly three hours later we were free to go. Since I'd been blocking the exit, I was the first one out.

Five miles down the road I started shaking so badly I could hardly hold the wheel. Then I thought about all the unusual things that had to happen for me to be at that place at that time, and about my church friends praying for me that evening. And I thought about my son, Ron, who'd led me to that church.

I looked in my rearview mirror at the line of trucks behind me and remembered leading another line of semis ten days earlier. I remembered the circle of truckers and their families, holding hands, voices joined together to pray, "Deliver us from evil."

a LITTLE BOY'S PRAYER

Shirley Corder

"What's the matter, Sweetie?" I lowered myself onto the bed next to my nine-year-old son, Stephen. His dark brown eyes glistened as he looked at me through swollen eyelids. Tears coursed down his gaunt cheeks. I smoothed his untidy hair from his forehead. "Are you hurting somewhere?"

He rolled his head from side to side on his crumpled pillow.

"Then what's wrong?"

"I—I want to be well again," he spluttered.

This was the child's second bout of Rheumatic Fever. The first episode, at age seven, kept him confined to bed for four months. This time he had already been at bed-rest for six months. To make matters worse, his six-year-old brother, David, had been diagnosed with the same disease a few weeks before. The doctors couldn't understand why both children had the same disease, but the blood tests were indisputable.

I slipped next door to David's room to make sure he had something to keep himself busy. We had tried putting the two children in the same room, but it didn't work. Stephen, our dreamer, wanted peace and quiet. He could amuse himself and rarely needed company. David's nature rebelled against the concept of rest. He wanted music, noise, games, and entertainment all day long.

With relief, I saw David propped up with his headphones on, listening to a story while he colored. I went back to Stephen.

After a few minutes of chatting, he asked me, "Mummy, why doesn't God make me well? Do you think He's cross with me?"

"Of course not. Why would He be cross? He loves you."

Stephen chewed stared out the window. "Then why doesn't He show it?"

I shot an emergency prayer heavenward as I sought the right words to help my little boy.

"Stephen, we have to keep praying that you'll get well soon, and that God will answer our prayers."

"He won't answer my prayers. I'm still little."

I tried to reassure him. "He especially loves children. Of course He hears your prayers."

"So can I ask Him for something, and He'll give it to me?"

I swallowed, sensing dangerous territory. "Steve, He will answer. But we have to trust Him to know what's best for us."

He looked at me intently and said, "I know what'll be good for all of us."

"What's that?"

"I want to go on a holiday. I want to be well, and to be able to swim in the sea and play in the sand."

My heart seemed to miss a beat. Financially, a vacation like that was not possible. We lived in landlocked Zimbabwe. We drove a small R4 that belonged to the church that my husband pastored. The tiny four-seater was already a squash for us and our three children. Even if we had the money, we couldn't drive 820 miles to the sea.

"Well then let's pray for that. Let's pray that we can all go together on a holiday to the sea," I responded.

Stephen's eyes lit up. "You think God can do that?"

"Absolutely," I replied with more confidence than I felt. "God can do anything."

"How will we get there?"

"We'll have to fly."

"Do we have enough money?"

"No, but God does." *Oh help. Lord, are You listening?*

My son's eyes shone with the first excitement I'd seen for months. "When can we go?"

"Well, we need to give God a chance to make plans," I blustered. "In any case, you don't want to go now. You wouldn't enjoy it. So the first step is to get well."

"And David."

"And David," I agreed.

"Can we tell everyone?"

I imagined the letdown the other two children would feel if God didn't come through. Stephen would be a big enough challenge. I knew God could do it, but I couldn't see *why* He would.

"Tell you what, let's make this our special secret," I suggested. "Just you and me."

"Not even Daddy?" His eyes gleamed at the thought of us planning the whole thing with only God knowing.

"At this stage," I agreed. "But the moment the Lord shows us His plans we have to tell Daddy, okay? Now you need to rest."

The noise in the next room revealed that my other son needed my attention.

"First we have to tell God," Stephen said. "He needs to know what we want."

We held hands and prayed. I simply, asked the Lord to give us all a desperately needed holiday. Stephen, however, was determined that God should know all the requirements. "Lord Jesus, we need to fly on a big plane," he explained. "And we'll need lots of money, because we need buckets and spades."

Over the next few days, every available moment, Stephen called me into his room and insisted that we pray more. Between those times of combined prayer, my own prayer-life went up 200 percent as I pleaded with the Lord to send a mighty miracle.

From the moment we agreed to pray this way, Stephen's health improved in bounds and so did his little brother's.

One evening, my husband answered the phone. He walked into the room some minutes later with a bemused expression.

"That was Charlie Gordon from the Durban North Presbyterian Church in South Africa," he explained. "A member of his congregation has come into money. He asked Charlie if he knows a minister and family who need a holiday at the sea."

My heart bumped. Charlie didn't know us well.

"So why did he phone you?"

Rob shook his head in amazement. "He'd read about the boys on a prayer list. He wanted to know if we would like a two-week holiday at the coast, staying in a luxury hotel."

My jaw dropped. "I can't believe it!"

I told him how Stephen and I had been praying for a holiday at the beach. He chuckled when I said I felt guilty for not telling him and reassured me, "I'm glad you didn't. I would have thought you'd gone crazy."

The next day we sat in Stephen's bedroom and told the excited little boy about the phone call. We then told our other two children. Then we all prayed together, thanking God.

Within a few weeks, the doctor said the children could get out of bed. To our disappointment, neither could walk. We rented wheelchairs and told Charlie to make our bookings.

Although the children were wildly excited, Rob and I still had concerns. The boys' illness had depleted our funds. We had no spending money. And since we were flying, we'd have no transportation in Durban. Without money, we wouldn't be able to get around.

Stephen continued to pray each day, reminding the Lord we would need "lots of money" to pay for a good holiday.

"Stephen, you mustn't be greedy," I said more than once. "The Lord is giving us this wonderful holiday. We don't need money to enjoy ourselves."

The child smiled and assured me we indeed needed "lots of money," and that the Lord understood.

At last the day dawned. We walked onto the runway toward the large South African Airways plane. Rob and I each pushed a wheelchair while our daughter, Debbie, bounced next to us.

When we landed in Durban, Charles and his wife, Sheila, met us and drove us to the beautiful Blue Dolphin Hotel perched high on a hill. We saw the white sandy beach far below. My heart sank. How would we get the boys down to the sand?

We walked into the hotel pushing the wheelchairs. Then Charles stretched out his hand to Rob. "Here are the keys for your car for the next two weeks." Tears filled my eyes as we expressed our gratitude. Charles brushed our thanks to one side, then handed Rob a thick envelope.

"And here's your spending money."

He then turned to the beaming children.

He grinned at them. "If you guys are going to have a good holiday, I just know you'll need lots of money of your own." He handed each a large bag full of silver coins. "With these coins you can play on the machines in the children's game lounge," he explained. "It's all yours, so enjoy it just as you want."

Stephen shot me a sideways beam as he thanked the man.

That afternoon, we went to the beach. We struggled down steep steps carved out of the rocky face, Rob and I each supporting a wheelchair.

When we eventually made it to the beach, we walked our boys carefully into the sea. They clung to us for support as the waves lapped around their wobbly feet. We then lowered them to a sitting position, and they sat splashing each other and laughing with glee.

If we thought going down was tough, climbing back was a nightmare. I didn't think we'd ever make it to the top.

The next day, we linked our hands and formed a chair lift. We carried first one boy then the next down the steep steps and lowered them into the water. By the third day, each of the boys could stand alone in the water. The waves on their ankles provided massage better than any physiotherapist could give them.

At the end of the first week, the boys could hobble down and back up the steep steps with our support. They bounced on the trampoline in the hotel gardens. Color returned to their cheeks.

Each day, we climbed into the car and went for a drive. After a few days Rob remarked, "Tomorrow we need to fill the car with gas." But the next morning, the car was full. We didn't spend a cent on that car in two weeks. Someone had taken it when we were in our rooms and filled it for us.

The children loved the machines Charles had referred to. The games were just right for their age. After a few tries, Debbie decided she'd rather save the money and spend it on something more lasting. Stephen and David both spent more on games, but then they too decided to see what the shops had to offer.

So two days before we returned home, we drove into Durban to a large shopping mall. There the children spent a wonderful time wandering around the first toy shop they had ever seen.

When the time came to climb on the plane once more, the wheelchairs went into the hold with our suitcases.

Back home, when we emerged from the arrivals hall, the friends who came to meet us let out a loud cheer as the two boys walked ahead of us. They each pushed their wheelchairs through the door with grins that told the whole story.

Truly, God had heard and abundantly answered a little boy's heartfelt prayers.

FIRE *on the* MOUNTAIN

Pamela J. Caldwell

Slowly my car climbed the mountain. My breath was shallow; my stomach fluttered. As I edged closer to the little hamlet of Running Springs, California, I anticipated the devastation I would see. This was the first time anyone had been allowed on the mountain since the fires had broken out ten days earlier.

During those ten days, I kept my eyes glued to the television news and the Internet blogs. I had reason for concern; I owned four rental houses in on-fire neighborhoods. For several days I was so distraught over the damage that was happening before my eyes and over the fear that friends might lose their homes or lives, I called my office and tearfully informed them that I was taking a few days off.

Lord, please, please stop these fires. Give the firefighters courage as well as strength to stay on top of the flames. Protect everyone.

My blue, two-story, hillside rental house's family had moved in only three weeks earlier—an eight-year-old, a dad, and a mom suffering with ovarian cancer. My old white cottage was home to a sweet husband and wife who struggled with marriage issues and finances. The yellow gully cabin was vacant, coming back after a massive flood from a broken pipe. The little brown cabin held my personal possessions until the new tenant's arrival. He was an older, single man who had epilepsy and a "working" dog.

The firefighters announced a mandatory evacuation as I kept praying for the safety of my tenants, who had less than an hour to pack a lifetime of memories into their cars and leave the mountain. *And of course, Lord, please keep my property safe.*

I knew the damage was awesome in the Running Springs area, with 201 homes burned to the ground. I thought all my rentals were still standing. But what I discovered when I reached the hilltop had a profound effect on my understanding of God, His sovereignty, and prayer.

We smelled smoke all over Southern California during those fires of 2007. But as I moved farther into the mountain area, my nostrils and eyes burned and watered. About a mile out of town, the charred remains of trees, shrubs, and homes lined the road. Tall, lone chimneys dotted the landscape. Memories filled my mind.

Years before, our growing family had spent many sunny, snowy days on the slopes skiing and sipping hot chocolate. As the grandchildren came along, we took out my childhood Radio Flyer sled to whoosh down the hills. After thirty years of marriage, I was divorced, so I bought my first cabin, a 1936 red clapboard home away from home, which became a place of respite and healing. Later, it was replaced with the little brown one.

The quaint shops and restaurants in town budded with new friendships. Because of the repairs I'd contracted when my home flooded, I knew many construction workers.

Now in the midst of desolation, I stopped at each rental house–first at those with tenants. The hillside cabin looked good. The neighbor showed me where the fire had whipped up the landscape, scorching the stair railings but nothing more. The old white cottage was a street away from any burn; it was safe. The gully cabin sat across from the main highway where the flames blew in the opposite direction; it was clear. Then I started to drive to the brown one.

As I drew closer to the cabin, my heart raced. *Lord, oh, Lord. How can this be?* Slowly pulling away from the stop sign at the top of the hill, I was not prepared for what I saw. As my car crawled toward the curve where the little brown cabin stood, the area was burned. The fire had raced up the hillside behind the house swallowing everything in sight. It destroyed the house behind mine. It moved down the street licking trees, engulfing houses, ruining lives.

South from the curve where my cabin stood, every house on both sides of the street was gone–more than twenty homes. I pulled into my driveway. *Lord, please take care of the people and help them with their losses.*

As I climbed out of my Rodeo, I saw how close the flames had come. Unbelievable! How was my house still standing?

I walked to the corner of the house and stood amazed. Blistered paint, scorched siding. A table had been thrown from the patio onto the hillside with its green paint blackened. A small antique window was stained with burn marks. Tree branches that once brushed the eaves were on the ground. Plastic planter boxes and pots now looked like giant, scorched Frisbees. Something had broken out a bedroom window.

Then I saw it. A large left hand print. What was that?

My neighbor to the north was standing on his porch. He called, "Amazing, isn't it?"

He explained, "I stayed until the last minute. I saw the firefighters under your deck. They kept the fires from moving in this direction. That handprint is the glove of one of them."

The firefighters had hunkered down and staid off the flames. The old shed that had stood less than 25 feet from the house was smoldering, completely gone, and yet somehow in God's grace my cabin still stood.

I tried to gather my thoughts. *Wow! Thank you, Lord! Thank you.* My mind whirled with many questions. How were my four houses, with seared handrails and melted shingles able to make it? Why did others lose everything and I lost nothing?

Could this miracle be attributed to answered prayer?

First Thessalonians 5:17 encourages us to pray continually. If there's one thing I did for those ten days, it was pray.

The desires of my heart were answered–my tenants were all safe, their possessions were safe and all my property was safe. My heart was sad for those who had lost so much, and I still shake my head and wonder, *Why?* I'd like to think that if the picture was different, if I were the one who had lost everything or had to start over; I could still find joy in the midst of the fire. For now, I will continue to praise Him and thank Him for my answered prayer.

a BULLET and a PRAYER

William H. Eastburn

The building where I practice law is a quaint eighteenth-century residence converted into office space. To get to my parking spot I drove under one hundred-year-old shade trees and past the carriage house where a county-seat judge once kept his horse and buggy. Embedded in a brick wall six feet above a neat bed of ivy, just to the right of my parking space is a bullet. It's not a relic of the Revolutionary or Civil War. It's from a .38 caliber revolver.

It lodged there a few years ago, just after it missed my head. Whenever I catch a glimpse of it I smile. Some might think it strange that a man would smile at a bullet, particularly one that narrowly missed his head. I might have thought this way myself—in fact, I'm sure I would have—before it was fired.

I've always been a type A sort. Being focused, and perhaps a bit compulsive, has helped me build a good law practice. My secretary used to confide that there were those in our office who found me forbidding and driven. I countered, "Well, maybe, but that's one way to get a lot done."

July 15 dawned with the promise of becoming a clear, lovely

summer day. My regular Bible study met in our renovated barn from 7:00 AM to 8:00 AM, as it does every Thursday. By 8:20 AM I had told Connie and one of our five children, Brooke, good-bye, and was on my way to the office. I was preoccupied because I had scheduled a conference that morning with clients who had flown in from several different states.

I pulled into my parking space at precisely 8:30 AM I stepped out of my car, slung my suit jacket over my shoulder, and was leaning back into the car to get my old leather briefcase when I noticed a gray Audi sedan had pulled in right behind me. Quickly, I glanced up and saw that the driver was a young woman I had represented a few months before; she had turned out to be mentally unstable. I had convinced her father to have her committed to a mental institution. When she learned this, she bought a gun to shoot me and "solve all her problems."

"When are you going to do something about my health?" she now screamed at me.

I took a deep breath.

"Mary, don't you remember? You fired me."

Before I heard the noise, I felt a bullet rip through the jack-et on my shoulder and smash into the wall. The report was still reverberating when the woman assumed a gunman's stance—feet wide apart and her revolver at arm's length steadied by both hands. Instinctively I raised my briefcase to shield my chest.

Blam! A bullet slammed through my briefcase and thudded sickeningly into my chest. I looked down. There was a crimson-ringed hole as big as a half dollar near my heart. Having worked on criminal cases, I knew about gunshot wounds.

That's it. I'm dead!

My chest was on fire. I felt as if the atmosphere had become a vise, squeezing my lungs so I couldn't take a breath. My legs collapsed as if there were no bones in them. My partners, Jay and Rusty, appeared at my side and lowered me the rest of the way to the pavement. They pressed against my chest to try to stop the bleeding. I was dimly aware of my assailant driving off and of a swirl of activity around me.

Lawyer that I am, I told my partners what had happened and who had shot me, since I knew a dying man's testimony is admissible in court. I said, "Tell Connie I love her."

Then I began to pray. "God, this is something I have no control over. I'm in your hands. Take over my life. Thy will be done."

What happened next was incredible. Right after my prayer, my fear and anxiety vanished. The pain stopped. I was wrapped in a feeling of total peace. During the next hour I remained conscious, talking with my partners and eventually with various doctors at Doylestown Hospital. Connie was soon by my side, and I smiled as she told me she loved me. When the trauma crew asked if they could cut off my trouser legs, I said, "Be my guest."

I could tell that people around me thought my behavior was strange. The medics assumed I was in shock. I was not. Once, when I was a college student, I was in the backseat of a car that smashed into a tree. I was thrown through the windshield, sustaining severe injuries. I was in shock then, so I knew what it felt like.

This was totally different. I wasn't in some woozy never-never land. I had surrendered myself completely to God, and I felt his presence. At the time I thought he was granting me a few lucid moments so I could be with my wife and partners before I died. It was a peace born of God, and truly it surpassed anything in my experience. I had never felt so complete, so at peace, so loved.

I was flown by helicopter to the University of Pennsylvania Hospital. There, doctors discovered the bullet had broken two ribs. It bruised my heart and took a nick out of my left ventricle, then punctured a lung before lodging in my back.

While recovering, I told my doctors I had been sure I was a goner. They agreed I had every reason to expect that. Before my three and a half hours of surgery, doctors had told my family I had only a 40 percent chance of surviving. However, my recovery was fast and complete.

Every day on the way into the office I see the bullet hole in the wall. For me it is a daily reminder of the ongoing miracle of God's love. Life is a gift, and for reasons I one day hope to understand, God chose to give mine back to me when it seemed it would be lost.

Before my experience, I never fully appreciated the message in Philippians 4:6, "Don't worry about anything; instead, pray about everything . . . ." How well I began to understand on that July 15. For when I surrendered myself in prayer, I experienced God's peace, just as Saint Paul promised in the next verse.

Maybe I'll always be type A—not happy unless I'm getting things done efficiently. But I can assure you that I now look on everyone I encounter as true gifts from God. One of the things I like to get done now is to know others better—slowing down so I can learn their priorities and concerns. No longer am I considered the resident dragon in my office.

I feel sympathy for the woman who shot me. She was committed to a psychiatric-care institution, and I pray she finds the peace I found on that July day when our paths crossed so dramatically.

After my recovery an associate joked that the act of shielding myself from a bullet was probably the most intelligent use any lawyer has ever made of his briefcase.

To his observation I might add that there's no better preparation for being shot than to come directly from Bible study.

SUCKER PUNCH

Tonya Brown

"I need to tell you something," my husband said after I crawled in bed and cuddled in his arms. Something in his voice made my body tense. "I have feelings for another woman."

Sucker punch. That one that you didn't see coming. The one that leaves you gasping for breath wondering, *Where in the world did that one come from?* and *How could I have been so stupid?*

I entered a battle that night that was not of my choosing. Not one that I saw coming. But I was in. The Bible tells us, "For we are not fighting flesh-and-blood enemies, but against evil rulers and authorities of the unseen world, against mighty powers in this dark world and against evil spirits in heavenly places" (Ephesians 6:12). Yet it sure felt like flesh and blood. His flesh. Her flesh. My bleeding heart.

I hate conflict. I cry "uncle" before anyone has a chance to even lay a finger on me. I've never been a fighter. I don't really know how to fight.

Spiritual warfare was a familiar term, but it was totally new territory for me. The feeling of rejection, now that was familiar to me. Of not being pretty enough, or sexy enough, or smart enough, or exciting enough. The enemy of my soul began hurling accusations into my heart and mind, and I believed every one of them. I couldn't compete with her. She was all of the things I was not.

I was about to lose the man I loved and my children were about to lose their father because I couldn't measure up. This realization left me gasping for air.

It reminded me of when I was a child and fell from a tree and landed on newly harvested corn stalk stubble. I feared that I might die then. I longed to die now.

In that cornfield years earlier, my older brother was there to walk me home. Since he'd had the wind knocked out of him before, he calmly explained what had happened to me. He also claimed that no matter how I felt at the moment, the fall was not fatal. He would walk with me until I could breathe again.

Now, pride and shame ganged up on me.

The last thing I wanted was for others to know. Yet, I knew I needed help. I could not handle this one alone. I desperately needed someone who had "been there, done that" to walk with me and assure me it wasn't fatal.

And just as my biological brother had been in that cornfield, a friend joined me on this battlefield. I had seen PJ at church, but had never met her. When our pastor told her about my situation, she agreed to meet and pray with me.

I wish I could say we met, prayed for my husband's change of heart, and he returned to me repentant that evening. I can't.

But I can say PJ and I hunkered down on our knees in the trenches of that spiritual battlefield and stormed the King's throne with our petitions. This woman's specific prayers startled me, and God's responses staggered me.

PJ spoke God's truth over the situation as she prayed with words from scripture. She reminded me that the King was enthralled with my beauty; that in Christ I was more than a conqueror; that all things could work for good; that He hated divorce; that God was for me. As these truths enveloped me, the fiery darts no longer hit their mark.

But that was only the beginning. She didn't stop there. She started asking God to work on my behalf. One time she prayed that God would minister to me through song. A few days later as I was driving into town, a song came on the local Christian radio station. I had never heard this song or the artist before, but it spoke strength into my soul. It said I would never be alone, and that even though I could feel the danger of the fight, angels would surround my soul! I accepted God's specific answer to PJ's specific prayer.

And the fight was long. Days led to weeks and weeks turned into months and still the affair raged. Few knew what was going on in our marriage. We donned our masks before Halloween ever rolled around and kept them on through Thanksgiving, Christmas, and into the New Year. Painted-on faces covered my tear-stained cheeks.

PJ and I continued to meet, and continued to pray over my situation and me. God continued to listen and to answer.

I was being guided by God's truth and I knew that my husband also needed to be hearing what God was saying about this affair. But he'd never been in the habit of reading his Bible, and he certainly wasn't turning there for answers now! He attended

Sunday services with me, but that was to keep up appearances. So as PJ prayed she asked God to speak to him through his dreams. I'd read about God doing that in the Bible, but did He still speak through dreams?

A few weeks later, my husband said, "I had the weirdest dream last night."

PJ's specific prayer; God's specific answer. A dream that spoke truth when my husband wasn't seeking it. A lesson for me that God is the same today as He was yesterday and that He'll be the same tomorrow.

PJ continued to pray, and I began to follow her example in my own prayers. My prayers became bolder and more specific as the air began to seep back into my lungs. I was starting to breathe again. I began to believe that I might survive. Maybe this wasn't fatal. I came to accept that even if my earthly marriage relationship ended, I would not be alone. I was learning what it meant to be the bride of Christ.

God hears and answers all of our prayers. This was a truth I had always believed. Now I not only believed it, I knew that it was true. I came to know other truths as well. I had to accept that He doesn't always answer with a "yes." Sometimes He says "no." And sometimes what we may presume to be a "no" may just be a "not yet."

I begged God to save and restore my marriage. A bold prayer. A prayer of faith. But after many months, I began to face the fact that this time the answer might very well be a "no."

My husband continued to live at home, attend church, and maintain an adulterous relationship. Under the wise counsel of our pastor, I finally said, "Enough is enough."

It was time for us to peel off the masks and for me to start exercising some tough love.

The decision was not at all an easy one to make and was even harder to implement. But I took a deep breath and issued an ultimatum to my husband: End the affair or move out of the house. I took a stand.

I was standing, but the effort was wearing me out. The struggle took its toll on me emotionally and physically. I lost weight. My blood pressure soared. I couldn't sleep at night and struggled to stay awake during the day. I was exhausted; yet the mask was off and it became easier to breathe.

During those months I repeatedly asked God to rescue me from this nightmare by taking me home to be with Him. I reasoned that my husband would be free to pursue a relationship that made him happy, and our children wouldn't be victims of their parents' divorce. It seemed like a good plan to me.

But God had a different plan.

His plan was to take what the enemy thought would destroy me, and use it to make me stronger—to teach me that my worth came from being the bride of Christ and a daughter of the King. I learned that what I really needed was for Him to fill this empty shell with the breath of life. I inhaled Him.

He soothed my soul first; then He changed my circumstances. His plan included my husband ending his affair. His plan offered me the opportunity to sit down face-to-face with the other woman and forgive my Christian sister.

And then His plan asked me to share my story not only with PJ, but also with others. He made it clear to me that this time I was to encourage others who were in the middle of a struggle with the spiritual forces of evil; to walk with them until they could breathe again. I was to share a story that declares that Almighty God not only listens to our prayers, but our loving Father also faithfully answers each of our prayers specifically. Each answer—whether yes, no, or later—breathing new life into each of His beloved children.

the ATV ANGEL

Stacy Voss

"Mom, you forgot to pray for Grandma." I was informed of this oversight before "Amen" even escaped my lips.

Three-year-old Micayla readily added people, animals, and just about anything else to her prayer list. Her list changed quickly. On Monday she prayed for the cat she saw climbing a tree. On Tuesday we lifted up her preschool teacher who seemed sad. Wednesday she asked God to protect her fish. Yet somehow Grandma was different. For a week straight, Micayla fervently prayed for her before breakfast, lunch, and dinner.

I've always longed for my daughter to grow into a woman of strong faith and to readily believe in the power of prayer. While I didn't want to diminish her enthusiasm, I secretly thought, *Again? There's not even anything wrong with Grandma.* My mom was in superb health and ran circles around me. She hadn't even had a cold in a while.

A few days and many prayers for Grandma later, I met a friend for coffee. We were lost in conversation when my phone rang. I pulled out my cell and looked at the screen. Mom.

Why's she calling me this early? It's not even 7:30 yet.

I knew my friend Kerri had to leave in five minutes, so I waited to call Mom back. As Kerri and I said our good-byes, my phone chimed to let me know I had a new voicemail. I listened to it as I started my car

"We were in an accident . . . air-lifted . . . hospital." The connection was clear, yet I couldn't understand her words.

My parents? In an accident? They were air-lifted? Wasn't that only for the most serious, life-threatening emergencies?

All the caffeine I had just consumed surged through my body and sent me on a singular mission: I needed to talk to my parents, immediately. I called my mom and anxiously waited for her to answer.

After the third ring Mom answered and cried, "Stacy, I'm sorry to have told you that on your voicemail. It's just that . . ." Her words trailed off as the tears unleashed their fury.

I don't recall her exact words. I just remember seeing cars drive by, people on their cell phones or singing. People acting as if nothing had happened. But something had. And it involved my parents.

"Dad and I went to visit Kathy and Daryl. We were riding their ATV when it flipped over. We were in the middle of the forest, so the ambulance couldn't reach us. We had to be air-lifted . . . Dad dislocated his shoulder and I'm bruised, but we'll be okay." Her voice quivered.

Time seemed to stand still before my parents were released from the hospital and friends brought them home. I waited for them, hoping to help. The front door opened and Dad walked in, his arm in a sling and his face forlorn. Behind him came my mom. Her right eye was nearly swollen shut, with only a sliver of crimson poking through in stark contrast to her violet and purple face.

"We were following Kathy and Daryl up the mountain. Mom was sitting behind me on the ATV," my dad explained in a monotone voice. "We came to a steep incline and I gunned it. The ATV went straight up. I pushed myself to the side so I wouldn't land on Mom. Then it flipped backwards, throwing Mom down the hill. I looked down and . . ." His voice trailed off. He had looked down the mountain and knew that his high school sweetheart and the love of his life was dead, pinned beneath the huge machine.

"No, Rick," my mom interjected. "You didn't get thrown to the side. You were there by me. The ATV was about to land on me. The front end with the weighty engine was heading straight for me. You pushed it just enough to push the heaviest part past me. I was pinned under the seat, which gave me a lot more space without being crushed."

"Nancy, I know you ended up under the cab. But there's no way I pushed the ATV. I was up the hill at least five feet from you," Dad argued.

"But I saw you. That's how you dislocated your shoulder."

"I landed on my shoulder when I fell off the ATV," my dad said. "It's not possible . . ."

"But I saw you there," my mom repeated emphatically.

My dad is an engineer. If he says something is physically impossible, I believe him. Plus, my mom said he saved her life. I'm sure he would take credit for such a feat if it were really true. And yet the earnestness on his face assured me it was not. Yet I can't believe my mom would alter a story, especially one that explains how she escaped a near-fatal accident with only bruises.

I can only think of one answer that bridges my parents' versions of the event. My dad threw himself off the ATV as he claims, landing with such force that his shoulder popped from its socket.

My mom fell down the mountain as she remembers. The ATV came tumbling after her and, moments before it crushed her, someone shoved it enough to prevent the engine from landing directly on top of her. Someone other than my dad.

Perhaps it was a direct intervention from God. Maybe it was an angel. I don't know. All I know is that my mom's life was spared by a matter of inches. I also know that if Micayla, or anyone else for that matter, asks me to pray, I will.

JUST *a* BLOCK *of* CHEESE

Stephen Clover

Our social worker at the welfare office promised help if we needed it. They told me we would be looked after. We believed them. But three aidless months had now gone by.

It was Christmas, when goodwill and peace abound. December being a busy month, tensions can run high; but we could handle it. The trouble was that we would be on the cutting edge to take care of our family.

I got very little holiday pay because I had only been working a few months. The factory was to be closed for a month over Christmas, and that wasn't good news for our family.

My wife and I went down to see the welfare agency. They didn't want to know us. We tried to explain our situation. It was like talking to a brick wall.

"You're working now," they explained to me. "You're no longer eligible for assistance."

"But I pay my taxes. I vote. The police don't live outside my house," I silently protested. Back at home the phone rang. It was my wife's sister. She was calling to let us know she and her three children would love to stay with us over Christmas. I was about ready to tear my hair out, wondering how we would feed them.

The opening line of an old hymn entered my mind: "Oh God our help in ages past." I knew only God could help us in this predicament of our family and extended family gathering and no resources.

My sister-in-law and her children arrived the night before Christmas and we had a ball. We decided that nothing would spoil our family gathering.

We decided to eat, drink, and be merry. Our children were happy. Why let money interfere with our festivities? Nonetheless our situation was tight. We used wisdom by adding extra water in the stew. More flour went in the beans. When the sugar ran out, the honey we had on hand became a substitute.

Then there are those priceless gems at the back of the pantry: items like ingredients for some dish you only made once. We pulled out the half empty bags of food that hadn't seen the light of day for a long time. They all went.

By the grace of God and sheer tenacity we made it through to the third week. My sister-in-law helped where she could. Being a single parent had put limits on her, too.

As the food and money did start to run out, in our family devotions we put more emphasis on asking for God to look out for us.

One day I felt led to write out a shopping list. None of us had any money. We just knew that God would provide. Without being flippant or over confident, I asked our family what groceries we needed: butter, tomatoes, lettuce, bread, flour.

Then my wife said she wanted a block of cheese.

"That is not a need," I explained to her. "It's a want. This list is for needs. Food needs."

"I don't care," she said. "I want a block of cheese."

Being a good husband I wrote it on the list. Honestly, mainly just to shut her up! Enough tension filled the house without our bickering on top of it! If we were going to have a row, I'd rather wait for something worthwhile to fight over—certainly not a block of cheese.

I opened the Bible at no particular place. The list went on top, and then we all laid hands on it.

The children in the house who wanted to pray did so. The adults then asked God to provide. We then thanked Him for what we were about to receive.

Three days passed with no answer. No knocks on the door. Not even any visitors. No angels. No money in the mailbox. We received nothing.

We were down to eating flour and water mixed in a paste. When we got tired of that we fried it in fat. Thankfully, it was a big bag of flour. Even better the factory was due to open again.

I knew I had some wages due but it was only for two days or so. It wouldn't be much. But it would be something. I went to work and did my eight hours for the man.

At the end of my shift I was getting in the van to come home. In my pocket were the few measly dollars the pay clerk had given me. I was thinking about how to spend them wisely.

Then the factory owner's secretary waved out to me. She showed me some boxes of groceries and said they were for me.

After thanking her I placed the boxes in our van. At home I parked my car and sat there in the car, reflecting on the food. My wife came outside to see why I hadn't come in the house. She climbed in the van and I told her what had happened.

We took the boxes inside and showed them to the family. Together we began opening them. Everything on that list we prayed for was there. And right on top of one box was a family-sized block of cheese.

"I'LL ALWAYS *be* HERE"

Guillerma Merancio
as told to Lupe Ruiz Flores

Even though our large family was scattered around the Southwest, from early on my granddaughter Claudia and I had a special bond. The drive from Tucson to her home in Texas was long and tiring, but when Claudia came running, her toddler legs surprisingly strong and swift, straight into my arms, I would feel full of energy again.

"Mama Mema!" she'd exclaim. We'd hardly spend a second apart for the rest of my visit. Claudia would be at my side in the kitchen and in church, and slept snuggled against me at night.

There was no question who would stay with her when she was rushed to the hospital with meningitis at age four while her mother, my daughter Maria, was pregnant. I planted myself at Claudia's bedside. I wanted to be sure that when she woke from her fever, she would look upon the face of someone who loved her. For days, she tossed fitfully, her eyes glazed and unseeing. I held her hand and tried to soothe her. "Rest, *mi'ja.* I am here for you always," I whispered; then prayed to God to take away my granddaughter's pain and give me a chance to keep my promise.

Finally one day Claudia looked at me and knew me again. "Mama Mema," she said, lacing her fingers through mine.

It was always like that between us when Claudia was a child—so much closeness, so much love. She didn't have it easy at home, even after her parents moved their family to Las Vegas for better jobs at the big hotels. Her father succumbed to drugs and was in and out of jail, and her mother struggled to support the family, working long hours as a hotel housekeeper. I could see when I visited that the east Las Vegas housing projects were not the best places for children. To my relief little Claudia seemed to be untouched by what went on there. She remained a bright and affectionate girl.

Then her parents divorced, and her mother remarried. Sadly, Claudia could not get along with her stepfather. By junior high, she was skipping school and sneaking out at night.

My daughter called me often. "I don't know what to do about Claudia," she explained. "She's been hanging around with some tough kids, getting into fights. I try to tell her they're not a good influence, but she won't listen to a word I say anymore."

"Be strong, Maria. She needs you," I replied. I wanted to go help my daughter and granddaughter. But by then my husband had suffered a stroke that made travel impossible for us. All I could do for Claudia from a distance was to keep praying for her.

One night just before Claudia turned 14, her mother called me. She was desperate. "It's more than a rough crowd Claudia's with. She's in a gang!"

My grip tightened on the receiver. *God, how did things in the family get so broken down that my granddaughter feels the only place she belongs is a gang?* My heart cried.

"A rival gang chased her home last night. They yelled for her to come out and wouldn't leave until the police came." My daughter broke into sobs. "Those kids swore they'd kill Claudia! I need to get her away from here."

"Bring Claudia to Tucson," I said. "I will look after her."

With its own share of drug deals and shootings, my neighborhood in the barrio was not much of an improvement on theirs, but at least Claudia would be safe from the gang. And maybe I could give her the attention she needed to feel like part of the family again.

My daughter warned me how much Claudia had changed. But nothing could have prepared me for the tall, sullen teenager who arrived at my door one February afternoon. No hug, no "Mama Mema." Instead, a defiant stare, baggy pants that dragged in the dirt, and an attitude even blacker than the lipstick smeared across her lips. This was not the Claudia I knew.

When her mother had to return to her younger children and her job in Las Vegas, Claudia's anger boiled over. "I hate it here!" she burst out one day. "There's no one to hang out with. How could Mom do this to me?"

"Claudia, your mother did this for your own good," I said.

"Why did she make me leave all my friends then?" Claudia asked. "They're the only ones who really care about me."

"*Mi'ja,* that's not true." I was going to add that her mother and I wanted only the best for her, but she stormed away.

"Oh, Claudia," I wanted to cry, "I can tell you need love. Why do you shut me out?"

Instead of our old closeness, a canyon of silence loomed between us. I could see Claudia on the other side, lonely and hurt and angry, and I longed to reach out my arms and pull her close to me again.

But I couldn't get through to her. She refused to make conversation; I talked to her anyway. I cooked her favorite meals. I set rules about schoolwork and curfew so she would know I had high expectations for her. I asked her to help me around the house. I wanted her to know she was needed.

Claudia didn't talk back to me, didn't put up a big fight when I woke her on Sunday mornings and dragged her to church, but she didn't listen to me either. Especially after she fell in with a group of kids who had her staying out until all hours.

I shuddered to think of what they were getting into. I'd seen what the streets could do to young people in the barrio, turning them old before their time, crushing their hopes in a way not even the hard life I'd known growing up in a poor Mexican village could do.

I almost wore a path in the kitchen floor with all my pacing and praying, waiting up for my granddaughter night after night.

"God, bring Claudia back safely," I would plead. "Let her see that my home and my heart are always open to her."

But when Claudia stumbled in and I asked where she had been, she would not even bother to brush her hair out of her eyes so she could look at me and give me a straight answer.

"Maybe you don't care what happens to yourself," I'd say as she hurried to her room. "But I do. I worry about you."

The rest of the semester, Claudia gave me cause for nothing but worry with her broken curfews and plummeting grades. Then one evening before school let out for the summer, she surprised me by joining her grandfather and me for dinner.

"The school's giving modeling classes this summer." For once, Claudia had started a conversation.

"Oh, really?" I tried to sound casual. "Would you like to go?"

"Yeah," she said, and then looked down at her plate. "But it costs money."

"Don't worry about the money," I said. *Maybe, Lord, modeling will help Claudia feel better about herself.* "We'll come up with a way for you to go."

"Really?" Her eyes flickered with an excitement even her practiced toughness couldn't conceal, and I knew that I would see to it my granddaughter took these classes that were so important to her. To cover the tuition, my husband and I used our savings, and Claudia's aunts and uncles pitched in, too.

The modeling course had Claudia eager to go to school, and I hoped this would extend to her other classes in the fall. She stayed home more at night, trying out different outfits and hairstyles. As the summer passed, her baggy pants were replaced by dresses. She pulled her hair back neatly and stopped using the black lipstick. I was thrilled to see the transformation in Claudia, especially the new confidence in her walk.

But when she started her freshman year at Desert View High School, I realized the change didn't go as deeply as I'd hoped. She made friends with kids that even she knew better than to bring home—the ones who grow up to be the kind of people you steer clear of on the street because their eyes are as cold and dead as their dreams.

How could I rest when my granddaughter was in danger of becoming like that? I was back to pacing the kitchen at night until she came home.

"Not again," she muttered once when she saw me waiting up for her.

"Claudia, where were you?"

She started walking down the hall.

I followed, saying, "I ask only because I worry about you."

"Well, I can take care of myself just fine," Claudia said. "Why won't you just give up, Mama?" She went into her room quickly and closed the door.

"I could never give up on you," I said, clinging to the fact that she'd called me Mama. Maybe I had touched, just barely, a part of the Claudia I once knew. "Don't you see that, mi'ja?"

She didn't respond. So I went to God. Even if I couldn't reach my granddaughter, maybe he could.

"Lord," I asked, "please tell Claudia for me: 'It breaks my heart that you go around like someone who has not a hope in the world. You have so much. You have the good mind and strong body God gave you. You have people who love you.'"

"Be strong," I told myself as I had once told my daughter.

One night early in the new year, I waited up for Claudia until I was nearly sick with anxiety. When she finally walked in, I broke down. "Claudia, this can't go on. I'm terrified you're throwing your life away on the streets." My tears spilled over. "The thought of losing you . . ." I covered my face with my hands. "I can't take it. I love you too much."

The only sound in the kitchen was my own crying. But when I caught my breath again and looked up, I saw Claudia's eyes filling with tears. Her whole body started shaking with sobs.

I reached out. Sighing, she fell into my arms. "I'm sorry, Mama," she whispered. "I don't want you to hurt for me."

"I don't want you to hurt anymore either," I said. "I know it might seem that your family let you down. But give us a chance. We'll show you we are still here for you."

I stroked her hair. "*Mi'ja,* I will always be here to love you."

Claudia wept, wetting my blouse with her tears as if she were letting out all the feelings she'd kept inside. Long after all of her tears stopped flowing, we held each other, until the canyon of silence between us disappeared into our embrace.

That Sunday Claudia was dressed for church before I was. I couldn't help sneaking glances at her sitting beside me, listening to the sermon. *Thank you, God, that my granddaughter has come back to me.*

For the first time since she came to live with me, Claudia tried to make a new life for herself. She joined the youth choir at church and later moved to the adult choir.

"I know you like singing with the other kids, Claudia," I said. "Why did you switch?"

"I feel bad for the older folks, Mama. No one wants to join their choir, so I did to keep them company."

I hugged her. "Mi'ja, you have never made me more proud."

Claudia began to bring friends home after school, friends she was clearly pleased to have me meet. In the spring one of the girls talked her into trying out for the tennis team, even though she'd never played before.

"I'll drive you home after practice," her friend coaxed.

I gave my blessing and Claudia's uncle got her a used racket. "How did it go?" I asked Claudia after the first practice.

"I'd thought tennis was for wimps, but I like it. I'm not any good, though. I hit the balls all over the place."

"Keep trying," I said. "You'll get better, I know it."

Claudia spent hours on the tennis court practicing. One day she came home so excited. "I made the team!" she cried. "The coach said he just couldn't turn down someone as motivated as I am. He told me I have a lot of potential."

Still Claudia's tone was tentative, reminding me that she was just beginning to learn to believe in herself.

When her friend dropped out of tennis, I worried she might take a step back, but the coach took over driving her home after practice. Claudia introduced me to the man. "Mama, this is my coach, Stacy Haines."

His Spanish was not much better than my English, so we just shook hands. In his gaze, I saw a strength and sincerity that I liked right away. I had a feeling Coach Haines would be good for my granddaughter.

He turned out to be great for her—for her tennis, and more important, for her self-confidence. He got her working as hard on her studies as she did on the court, and by the spring of her junior year, she had made the honor roll.

"Coach said if I keep improving my grades along with my game, I might get a scholarship to college," Claudia told me one night as she sat down to study after dinner. "College, Mama, can you believe that?"

"With hard work and with God, I believe you can do anything, *mi'ja.*"

The smile my granddaughter gave me could have lit up the entire desert sky, and I thought, *This is the Claudia I know!*

This is the young woman I knew was there beneath the gang-girl façade and the one I could not give up hope on: the one who graduated as captain of the Desert View High tennis team and as Tucson's Student-Athlete of the Year. She made her coach and family proud as a tennis player and education major at Stetson University. I found the joy of watching her live up to the promise that God saw in her all along.

This is Claudia Meza, my granddaughter, who tells me every chance she gets, "I love you, Mama."

I have the feeling she knows what the answer in my heart is: *Not any more than I love you,* mi'ja.

MIRACLE *on* ROUTE 30

Connie K. Pombo

"Folks, make alternate plans if you're traveling west on Route 30. There's an injury accident," said the radio announcer.

Not again . . . I'll be late for Jeremy's game, I thought as I grabbed the cell phone and called my husband. "Honey, I'm tied up in traffic," I told him. "It looks like it will be a while, so go to Jeremy's game without me."

"Are you sure?" my husband replied.

"Yes. I heard on the radio that I'm waiting behind an injury accident and both lanes are blocked."

Just then I heard sirens and saw two ambulances pass in the opposite lane. If I could just make it a few hundred feet, the next exit would take me to another route that was longer, but would be quicker than sitting in traffic. Two cars ahead of me had the same plan, so I followed them.

Ahh, what a relief! Maybe I could make it to the last inning of Jeremy's baseball game after all.

As I drove on the overpass of the highway, I saw the accident. It looked like the car had rolled several times and landed upside down. I wondered if anyone could have possibly survived something so horrific.

I was moved to pray aloud, "Lord, please be with the people in that car, be with their families, and help the medical personnel attend to their needs."

Chills ran up my spine as if I were praying for my family. While I drove on, each time the image flashed in my mind, I prayed again.

Forty-five minutes later, I entered our driveway. Mark, my husband of 25 years, was waiting for me on the front steps.

That's odd, I thought. *I told him to meet me at the game.*

Mark ran to the car and shouted, "Move over! I'm driving!"

"Okay, not so fast, I need to change clothes first," I said.

"No, there's not enough time," he replied.

When I started to open the car door, Mark grabbed my hand and said, "I don't have time to explain. Just let me drive."

Mark had never spoken to me in that tone of voice!

"What's up with you anyway?" I questioned. As I gave Mark the car keys, I saw panic mixed with fear. Beads of sweat formed on his forehead and tears trickled down his cheeks.

Then, without a word, I knew. As I buckled my seat belt, I grabbed Mark's hand and prayed, "God, please help our son. Help the doctors and nurses who are working on him right now and let him be okay."

It was a parent's worst nightmare—when you hear the words, "I'm sorry, but your son has been in an unfortunate accident."

That was all the information Mark had received. We were back en route to the same hospital where I had just completed a double shift. I was still in my uniform as my husband sped out of the driveway. The way Mark was weaving in and out of traffic and ignoring traffic signals, made me realize we didn't have much time.

As Mark swerved into the hospital parking lot, we saw two ambulances with their lights still blaring.

"Go on. Get out. I'll park the car!" Mark shouted. I fumbled for the door handle. The blaring sirens followed me into the emergency room entrance where I stood in front of the receptionist. Her kind eyes met mine as she said, "Can I help you?"

Tears formed in my eyes. "My son. He's been in an accident!"

"His name?" she asked politely.

"Jeremy Pombo," I murmured.

My vision blurred as she passed a sign-in sheet through the sliding glass window. I wrote my name and waited for her reply.

"Just take a seat. Someone will be right with you," she said.

Although I had worked in the medical field for twenty years, I felt as if it were my first day. Everything felt foreign—the white tile, the antiseptic smell, and the swirling of green hospital garb. I felt nauseated. *Is this what it feels like to lose a child?* I thought.

"Mr. and Mrs. Pombo, you can come back now," said the receptionist. Mark wrapped his arm around me and I leaned hard against his chest. I waited by the nurse's station, while Mark signed more forms. The curtains were drawn to each emergency room cubicle, but I spotted a familiar object lying on the floor. I recognized it because I tripped over it every evening when I came home from work. It was Jeremy's tennis shoe.

I whispered, "Is that our son's shoe?"

Mark followed my gaze to the blood-splattered shoe and held me tightly. The emergency room doctor interrupted us, "I don't want to upset you, but your kids are pretty badly beaten up. There's a lot of blood, but mostly from facial lacerations. They're conscious and able to talk. You can see them now."

"Our kids?" I questioned.

"Yes, there were three in the accident—both your sons and a girlfriend, I believe."

My knees buckled and another wave of nausea washed over me as the ER doctor led us to the first cubicle.

When the curtain opened, I was not prepared. Jeremy's face was swollen beyond recognition and tears mixed with dirt and blood on his cheeks. He called, "Mom, is that you?"

"Yes, Jeremy, I'm here. The doctor said you'll be fine." As soon as I uttered the words, tears poured down my cheeks. Jeremy reached out his hand. "Mom, please don't cry!" I grabbed tightly to his bruised hand and choked out, "I prayed for you this afternoon and God answered my prayer."

A confused look crossed Jeremy's face and his eyes closed. The nurse came in to take his vitals and directed us to the next cubicle where Jon—our eleven-year-old son—was motionless. He was connected to a mesh of tubes and wires, but he was breathing on his own.

I brushed the matted hair from his face and kissed his forehead. "I prayed for you and you'll be okay, Jon. I love you," I whispered to him.

The last cubicle was empty. Jeremy's girlfriend, Kathy, had been taken to the X-ray department. Just then the orderly wheeled her back in the room. She had minor lacerations and a severely broken nose. Kathy smiled weakly and said, "I'm fine. Go be with Jeremy and Jon. My parents are on their way."

"It's a miracle they're all alive," Mark said, shaking his head. "I don't understand how it's possible."

"I do," I responded. "I prayed for them this afternoon."

Mark looked perplexed. "But you didn't even know they were in an accident." Mark's jaw quivered, "How did you know?"

"Remember when I called and said I would be late?" I asked.

Mark nodded.

"I was on Route 30 when the accident happened and saw the car from the overpass. Whenever I saw that image in my mind, I prayed for the families of the victims and the medical personnel. I had no idea that car contained our children, but God did and He answered my prayer," I explained.

Mark wrapped his arms around me and whispered, "God performed a miracle on Route 30."

Later we learned that a refrigerator fell off the back of a flatbed truck. Jeremy swerved to miss it and lost control of the car. The car flipped several times and landed in an embankment upside down with the roof caved in. The police officer said he'd never seen an accident so severe where all the victims survived.

Since then, when our family hears a siren, sees an ambulance, or gets stopped in traffic, we pray. We pray for the victims, their families, and the medical staff because we know the power of a single passionate prayer.

The key to Jeremy's Ford Escort was the only thing salvaged from the wreck. That key remains in the ash tray of Mark's car as a reminder of the prayer that saved our children's lives. On the key is the date of the accident and the words *Route 30*.

MY PRESCRIPTION *for* PRAYER

Ronnie J. Johnson

"You have a very serious condition called viral myocarditis."

"So how much longer until I get out of the hospital?"

"Look, you almost died. Your heart is enlarged and beating too fast. We'll keep you here for another week to watch."

My mind lost focus on the cardiologist as he explained that he had consulted with specialists concerning my case. Even lying in the cardiac-care unit hooked up to a transmitter that broadcasted my every heartbeat to concerned observers, I could only think about how I couldn't be sick for long.

In just a couple of weeks, I would make a proposal to my faculty advisory committee concerning my dissertation. For three years, I had struggled with such graduate school requirements as foreign language exams, comprehensive exams, and orals. Now the end was in sight; I only needed to write a dissertation. I would then have my Ph.D., and this highly stressful time in my life would be over.

"After you return home you must get complete bed rest for at least three months."

I snapped back to hear what the cardiologist was saying.

"I'll prescribe various medications but you must have complete rest, no activity whatsoever. You must stay in bed all day. You may go to the bathroom and perhaps to the kitchen table but no more than that. If you do not follow these instructions, you may die."

Nothing could have prepared me for that treatment–three months of complete bed rest! My heart jumped as my mind raced with the reasons I couldn't stay in bed for three months. I had to write a dissertation and get my Ph.D. Besides, I didn't feel bad unless I exerted myself or got excited–which I was doing just then, because a nurse rushed into the room and told the doctor that my heart rate had just sped to a dangerous level.

"Calm down. When you get emotional or do physical activity your heart beats like you are running a marathon. It will wear itself out if you do not let it rest."

He told me after I stayed in bed for three months I might be able to resume limited activity, but only if my heart improved.

"What about school?"

"You must drop out until your condition improves. Still be cautious because the stress could worsen your condition. If you follow instructions, you should be completely healed within a couple of years, possibly sooner, and then you can return to your graduate school."

A couple of years! The reality of what I had done to myself began to soak in. Even with counseling as my minor, I had failed to recognize my reaction to pressure. I had studied how stress could harm the human body by lowering its resistance to disease. I just never thought it would happen to me.

After the cardiologist left the room, I turned to the Great Physician in prayer.

"God, why did this happen to me?"

The answer wasn't immediate, but it became as clear as the diagnosis the cardiologist had just made.

I was only in graduate school in the first place to help me be a better minister. After I received a Master of Divinity, I worked as a chaplain intern at a state mental hospital. God gave me the desire to help people through Christian education and counseling. When I first moved to the university, I had joined a church and had gotten involved as a youth minister and Sunday school teacher. However, as I got busier with schoolwork, I did less at church. My relationship with God also suffered as I stopped spending time in prayer and Bible study.

You now have time to pray. This is the first time I have heard from you in quite a while, was the response I heard to my prayer.

That was the most important lesson I needed to learn. My desire to serve others had slowly been replaced by the desire to get the Ph.D. I reasoned that the sooner I got the degree, the sooner I could serve better. I thought my service to God and others would just have to wait until I finished school.

While in bed, I had plenty of time to spend with God. Bible study and quiet reflection didn't require much physical exertion. I got more spiritual exercise those three months than I had in the past three years.

I asked for forgiveness. Even though I was preparing to be a better servant, I still needed God in the present. Instead of trying to do it all in my own strength, I turned back to God and asked Him to use me, even if I never got my coveted Ph.D.

At my third month checkup, the cardiologist told me, "The ultrasound tests of your heart show that it is almost back to normal. You can begin some limited activity—going to the store, church, and such. But please take it easy."

I would take it easy because I was no longer in a great hurry to complete my degree program. God showed me in the three months of quiet reflection that He wanted me to simply focus on Him. I experienced important things with a renewed spirit. Sunday school, worship, and other church activities had new meaning now that I could do more than read about them in the church bulletin. With my renewed vision, I recognized that every small thing I had taken for granted was a gift from God.

At the one-year checkup, I heard the best words possible.

"Everything checks out normal. You've had a miraculous recovery. I'm taking you off your medications and we don't have to schedule any more appointments. I don't see why you can't do whatever you want from now on."

Soon after the doctor told me that my heart was healed, I received the opportunity to teach part-time at the seminary I had attended six years earlier. Then a small congregation asked me to be their pastor. I accepted every opportunity that God gave me to serve. While serving as professor and pastor, at times I experienced greater pressure than when I was in graduate school. However, my internal reaction was not the same. Physically, I accepted my limitations, emotionally I faced reality, and spiritually I depended on God for strength.

Proverbs 4:23 tells us, "Guard your heart above all else, for it determines the course of your life." In Solomon's day, the heart was thought to be more than the organ that pumps blood; it was the center of intellect, emotions, and the will. I had let my reaction to stress infect my heart with a virus that dried up the center point of my heart. Time alone with God had been the best prescription for my condition.

I received my Ph.D. five years later than I'd planned. My dissertation was completely different from the one I'd originally outlined. Instead of writing something just to complete my degree, I conducted a study to help my seminary integrate older-adult ministry into theological education. The findings still help me as a tenured professor.

Of course, the lesson God taught me through that tough, three-month prescription is even more useful–guard your heart and listen to God!

MY LITTLE JOB

Eva Juliuson

My little job may not have seemed very important to most people, but it worked just right for me that year. I was a part-time playground attendant.

My kids' elementary school had a difficult time filling the position. The job was in the middle of the day during the lunch recess time, so it was hard to combine with any other job. And the two hours each day at minimum wage certainly wouldn't pay bills. However, sometimes those two hours seemed like two whole days! It depended on the students' moods. Regardless, I can guarantee that I more than earned my little wage!

Each day I looped my whistle around my neck and loaded my belt pack with hall passes, Band-Aids, my walkie-talkie, and a notepad. Then I headed for the cafeteria to take the first group to the playground.

I could usually tell right away if it would be a tough day or not. Sometimes a haggard-looking teacher, who was thankful for the break, would sympathetically touch my arm to wish me luck. Then I knew I was really in for a challenge that day!

Most people who've been around more than one child know that when you put two or more kids together, you'll be in the middle of arguments, tattling, hurt feelings, and skinned knees. When one hundred third- through sixth-grade kids fill the same playground at one time, you can only imagine what a playground attendant can get hit with—literally and figuratively! Some days the entire student body seemed hyped up.

Standing in the middle of a hundred kids, trying to keep an eye on everyone at one time, something happened. I began to realize my enormous responsibility for each child's safety and well-being. The "mother" in me began to pray for them as I watched over them.

I noticed that the days I prayed on my way to work seemed to go smoother, so I began to pray every single day! I asked God to bring His peace over the whole school; to calm teachers' nerves (and mine!); to help the kids play with respect for one another; to help me reach the kids who needed someone; to give me wisdom in helping the kids work out their disagreements; and to be ready to show His love to every student and teacher.

The more I prayed over my little job, the more I saw God at work! It was exciting! So I prayed even more. I prayed for specific needs: such as the little boy who had no friends, or the teacher who always seemed to be in a bad mood, or the girl whose clothes were always a little too small, or the boy who seemed a little too street-wise.

I prayed for the friends who got into fights, for the banged-up elbows and beat-up egos, for the kids who were angry and ready to fight and those who were quiet. I prayed for the kids' families, and for the teachers, and for the janitors.

It was fun to pray and watch what God did in different situations. I learned to keep my eyes open for what to pray for and for ways God was answering.

One day after the last bell rang, I checked the playground for forgotten jackets and lunch boxes, and then headed inside to clock out. As I walked toward the office, I heard a whimper. A young girl sat in the hall. Her head was in her hands and she was trying not to cry.

"What's wrong?" I asked as I squatted beside her.

She burst into sobs. "I can't believe I did it! I never do bad things! I'm just so upset over what's going on at home!"

I placed my arm around her shoulders to calm her. She said her teacher had sent her to the hall for being mean to another student. The young girl obviously had a lot on her mind and needed to talk. Her teacher poked her head out of the classroom, gave me a look of gratitude, and left us alone in the hall.

I found out the girl's name was Samantha.

"My stepdad had to leave home because of something bad he did to my sister." The words tumbled out of her mouth. "She's all upset. My mommy won't stop crying! I want my stepdad back. I want everyone to be happy. I don't know what to do!"

After listening to her, I told Samantha that when I was upset talking to God helped me best. I explained that He knew everything that was going on and He could help her know what to do if she would ask Him for help.

I asked if I could pray with her. Then I asked if she, her mom, and her sister would like to come to our church. Her eyes lit up with hope. Samantha was sure her mom would because she had stayed up late the night before watching things about

God on TV. I wrote her mom a note, explaining who I was and that I had prayed with her daughter. I invited them to church and gave them my phone number. I hugged Samantha and walked her back to her class. Then I continued to pray for this broken-hearted little girl and her family.

At church the next Sunday, someone told me a lady was asking for me. There was Samantha standing next to her mom! The whole family began coming to church regularly. Samantha was baptized a month after I first met her on my job! My little job!

No job is insignificant when it is saturated with prayer! In fact, prayer can supernaturally equip us to be ready to reach out to others no matter where we are or what we are doing. It can cause any job to have eternal results!

SOMETHING *was* THERE

Paul D. Grams

The call came at 1:00 AM. on April 3. A two-story apartment building in the center of town. Flames in the basement and on the ground floor. Assigned to Ladder Company Number One, I rushed to the scene with my partners Ron and John.

I jumped out of the truck and glanced at the house, a turn-of-the-century building with wooden siding. Flames licked at the basement windows; the upper windows were blackened by smoke. After 14 years in the Rockford Fire Department I knew these dwellings well. Of basic wooden construction, they have nothing to slow a fire as it rises. We would have to act fast.

An elderly man ran toward us. "A woman lives up there with her grandson," he shouted. "On the second floor. You've got to get them out."

"Anyone downstairs?" I asked.

He shook his head. John and Ron broke the door down. The three of us put on our facemasks and air tanks and scrambled up the stairs. The air in our tanks would only last about 15 minutes.

The night was cool and damp with no wind, and smoke

hung in the apartment like a thick fog. My flashlight was only a few inches from my face, but I could barely see a dull glow. Lost in the pitch dark, we tried to stay in touch by voice.

"Ron, you there?" I asked. "John, is that you?"

"Yeah." The responses were muffled, muted; even sound was distorted by the smoke.

Crawling, I bumped into a coffee table, then an overstuffed sofa. I reached for the wall, and my fingers brushed a hanging plant. *Look to the floor,* I thought. In a fire children often hide, hoping to escape danger. I patted the rug under a chair.

"No one here," I finally shouted.

Methodically we searched. In the small home, everywhere we turned we encountered chairs, tables, houseplants, a TV.

We worked our way to the kitchen, linoleum beneath our hands. I felt my way under a table and inspected a closet. No one. Ron called from the bedroom, "The place looks empty." John confirmed from the dining room, "No one here."

Thank you, God, I prayed. *No one here. I hope they're safe.*

Now we had to get out. Through the thick black I spotted a finger of flame lapping up through a heating vent near my face.

"Let's go," I said.

We felt our way along the floor back to what we thought was the living room, but we couldn't be sure. We seemed to be in a maze. Which way was out? If we'd had the fire hose with us we could have followed it back out the door. The air was so still and cold that the smoke didn't move; we were trapped in darkness.

"Ladder Company Number One is on the second floor," Ron spoke into his radio. "We're lost. We need someone to ventilate the building immediately so we can find our way out."

Another crew was on the ground, hosing the fire on the first floor. If someone down there would break more windows maybe the air would clear.

We waited, breathing slowly, conserving our air supply. No one came. Nothing happened.

The warning bell on John's tank started ringing, signaling his air was low. Our time was running out.

I pulled out my radio. "Chief!" I shouted. "We are trapped on the second floor. We are lost in smoke and are almost out of air. Break the windows so we can find our way out. Now!"

No response. Somehow they weren't hearing us. I started crawling forward, straining to find the exit. An image came to me, a horrifying photo in a fire-fighting magazine I had recently read. The picture showed a firefighter's handprints on a wall, only inches from the window that would have let him out. The man died just a breath away from safety. *God, don't let the same thing happen to us.*

Just then I felt my shoulder bump into someone. "John, is that you?" I asked. No answer. "Ron, are you there?"

No answer. Who was it? Someone to rescue us?

I inched forward and bumped the same thing. It wasn't a piece of furniture; it was moving. And then a deep voice spoke, in a tone so cold that a chill ran through me: "You will never get out of here alive." It was as though evil incarnate had spoken.

No, you're wrong. I will get out of here! I thought of my wife at home praying. Whenever I was in trouble I clung to that image of Val bowing her head in bed or turning to a few pages of her Bible before she fell asleep. Her prayers had kept me safe before; surely they would do so again.

No, I will get out of here, I thought. I would not let fear take me over. *I will survive. God will help me.*

Suddenly I heard glass shattering. One of my partners must have found a window and broken it. I headed toward the sound and reached the window. A ladder appeared. John scrambled down to safety. I went next. As I climbed over the sill I sucked in the final breath of air left in my tank. Ron came last.

On the ground we took off our masks and gulped deep drafts of fresh air. The fire shot up through the building and the second story burst into flames only moments after we left it. We were alive, safe!

Back at the station we received confirmation that the people who lived in the apartment had not been home that night. I called Val and told her not to worry when she heard the news on the radio that morning. "Ron, John, and I got lost in dense smoke, but we're okay," I said. "I'll see you when I get off duty."

I casually asked Ron and John if I had bumped into them before we got out. No. They hadn't heard the voice and had no idea what I was talking about.

When I got home Val had already gone to work at the elementary school where she is the secretary. We spoke on the phone, and I described the horror of being lost and hearing that frightening voice. "Your prayers must have got me out of there," I told her.

"But, Honey," she said, "I was sound asleep when you telephoned. I hadn't been awake for several hours."

"You're kidding," I said.

"No," she insisted.

"Well, someone must have been praying," I said.

That day at work Val pondered my close call. She smiled hello when Sherry Zahorik, who works in the day-care program, came into the office. As Sherry started to tell the principal about her "strange night," Val gasped in astonishment.

With no previous knowledge of the situation I had been in the night before, Sherry told this amazing story:

"Sometime after 1:00 AM I awoke with such heaviness in my chest I could hardly breathe. I began praying as I recalled the dream I had just had. I could see three people in a dark room, trapped by thick smoke. These three people were crawling, frantically searching for something. I could feel confusion and a demonic presence permeating the room.

"Then this demonic presence laughed and said, 'You will never get out of here alive.' While the presence was speaking, I envisioned a picture of a fireman clawing at the wall, thinking it was a window.

"I got up and went into the living room, where I continued praying. Each time I thought it was safe to go back to bed, the heaviness returned. Finally the pressure was gone and I felt an extraordinary peace. I knew the crisis was over and everything was all right. I went back to bed and slept soundly."

When Val told me about Sherry's dream and her vigilant praying, I was stunned. Everything Sherry said corresponded to my experience the night before. I'm convinced her prayers protected me from an evil force that was so real I could touch it. I felt it right next to me, breathing, speaking, ready to extinguish all life—and then it was gone.

I have no doubt the extraordinary power of prayer can protect us from evil. And release us from the impenetrable dark.

HAPPY NEW YEAR

Yulia Bagwell

It was a typical celebration: guests, festive TV shows, eating, drinking, laughter, and anticipation. But for Bill, a pastor from Long Island, it wasn't.

Bill had traveled to Belarus with a team united by one mission: investigating the possibilities of adoption.

The team members were hosted in different places, and the pastor from Long Island was assigned to stay with a family who didn't know English. Bill's Russian wasn't very good either; so he frequently referred to a pocket dictionary. But even with the dictionary he couldn't understand what was going on at this ritual of late gathering he had to be part of.

"Yulia, what's going on here?" Bill exclaimed when he saw me. He and I were friends but hadn't seen each other for a year.

"It's a typical New Year's Eve celebration," I replied and joined the noisy crowd at the table.

"Yulia, now we have you to interpret for us and our guest," the middle age hostess announced. She added in a whisper, "He came yesterday, and we've had such difficulties communicating."

"Dah," Bill confirmed in Russian, as if he understood what the woman had said. Now he was happy, too: He had a personal interpreter. "What did she say?" he asked me.

Here we go! Whether it was New Year's or Easter, Sunday or Thursday–I always seemed to end up interpreting something for someone, any time Russians and English-speaking people mingled. Even while I ate, I still had to work–between bites and sips.

"Yulia, want some?" the host was eager to fill my glass full of his vodka.

"Oh no, thank you. I don't drink," I replied.

"We don't drink, either!" the guests thundered cheerfully. "We're just celebrating new beginnings: health, love, success!"

"Yulia, a little bit, of our favorite . . . Russian . . . famous!" the host tempted me with the sparkling crystal glass of vodka. Then he turned to the American and asked, "You want some?" The crowd's attention shifted to the pastor.

"No, thanks, I don't drink," Bill said indifferently.

"Is he a Baptist?" one of the guests winked at me.

"You aren't a Baptist, are you?" another one, already drunk, probed me.

"I am," I said with a smile.

"What?" The whole group dropped their forks.

"You can't be a Baptist!"

"You don't look like a dumb sect member."

"You're too young for that!"

The people's faces became sullen–in Belarus, being a Protestant Christian was a controversial issue. It was considered abnormal. Admitting you were a Baptist invited judgment and condemnation.

Finally, someone broke the awkward silence and said, "Yulia, ask our dear friend: Is it common in America to believe in God?" While translating the question, I noticed the tension.

"Yeah," Bill answered. "It's common." His answer electrified the crowd. "And it's common to go to church. We also have Christian radio and TV, movies, books, magazines . . . ."

"Wow," everyone breathed out. "It's so different there!"

"Can't you go to church?" Bill asked.

"You know, Bill," the hostess answered. "We don't believe in God. But my children attend a privileged school where the Holy Book is taught," she explained proudly.

"Can't you study the Bible?" Bill asked.

"Are you kidding me?" She giggled nervously. "I hold such a post! I don't want to lose my job. I don't mind if my children study the Bible, but it's not for me."

"But what if something happens to you tonight?" The pastor kept trying.

"Bill, Yulia, let's change the subject." The hostess's husband got uncomfortable. "Tonight we're celebrating the New Year's beginning. So let's have a drink: Happy New Year, everyone!"

The folks were ready for another shot of alcohol and excitement. They weren't interested in the pastor's evangelism. From then on celebrating spiraled to dramatic binging.

Observing the carouse of "new beginnings," the American pastor left for his room. As much as I liked the holiday, I got embarrassed and left, too.

In the morning Bill and I, as well as his team and other interpreters, visited an orphanage. A prison-type building, the overworked teachers and the kids with eyes full of heartbreak and longing made quite a depressing impression on us. Bill and I were more than relieved to get back to his temporary home.

While the hostess cooked and the host quietly did his work, Bill and I relaxed and talked.

"Yulia, do you happen to know if we're going to eat here or go out?" Bill asked.

"She's fixing the lunch," I replied. "I guess we're eating here. Actually, in Belarus people eat at home most of the time. Besides, everything is closed today."

"I see. I'm getting hungry," my friend confessed, as he inhaled the aroma of the homemade meal.

The hostess came out of the kitchen. Ignoring our friendly comments, she slipped into her bedroom. Her husband followed her. Bill and I kept talking.

The host walked back. Today he seemed to be a nice guy, just not a believer. I heard him dialing the telephone.

The couple's sweet kids, a boy and a girl, quietly joined us, as the host went back to the bedroom, and then returned to the telephone. Then he rushed back to the bedroom.

"Yulia, what's wrong?" Bill asked me, watching the man.

"Victor," I addressed the host, as he ran through the living room. "Are you alright?"

"Alright, alright," Victor mumbled.

"Victor, are you hungry?" Bill asked the host with humor. Victor's reaction was hard to interpret. "Yulia, why's he so strung?" Bill asked. I had no idea.

"Victor, what's your wife doing?" I questioned, thinking about the lunch we hadn't eaten yet.

"What she doing?" he echoed hysterically. "Dying!"

"What?" we exclaimed in unison. "You are joking!"

"Children, stay here. Yulia, please, comfort them!" The host was not joking. The man was frightened. "What to do?"

"Victor, call 911 or whatever you call it here," Bill suggested.

"Ambulance? What ambulance?" Victor almost yelled at the American. "Don't you understand? Today is January 1! Everything is closed!" Victor was losing his nerve.

"But if she's dying, something must be done." Bill tried to sound calm. "Yulia, in my country I'd call 911. What do you do here?" The pastor looked perplexed.

Pray, I thought.

"Oh . . . please. Someone . . . help!" Victor panicked. "She's dying! Dying! I can't help her!"

"Bill, can we pray?"

"Yulia, she needs a doctor!" Bill replied, frantically.

"But doctors are drunk! Could we pray?"

"We need to do something besides pray," Bill argued. "I'll call a doctor from my team!"

He dialed the number. No success. "Yulia, we need to do something," Bill urged, while looking at the crying kids.

"Bill, let's pray!" I said again.

"But these people don't even believe in God!"

"Bill, Bill, please. Please," Victor was gasping, running around. "Please, can you pray for my wife?"

"But, Victor, I thought you . . . I thought that you don't believe in God." The American was confused.

"Please, Yulia! Yulia, ask him to pray. Please! Yulia, Bill, go ahead. Pray for my wife," the man frantically dialed the ambulance number over and over. No success.

At last, Bill agreed to say a prayer. Was it brief! I almost yelled at my friend, begging him to go on.

"She's dying!" Bill reacted in frustration. "She needs an ambulance!" Knowing the helplessness of the situation, I still pushed him to pray.

What to do?

The kids sobbed . . . .

What to do?

I began to mumble my prayer.

Honestly, my prayer had no logical consistency. Whatever was boiling in my heart, I was inwardly, passionately pouring before God.

"God, why is she dying?" "Jesus, she's not ready!" "God, what am I supposed to do?" "Lord, come, come quickly." "Jesus, no ambulance today, don't you know that?"

Victor faithfully moved from the dying wife in the bedroom to the hopeless phone in the hall. Kids wept. Bill looked lost.

What to do?

"God, help!" I cried. The doorbell rang. Victor sprang to open it. People in the white robes followed the man.

"Who are these?" Bill asked me, glancing at the strangers. My mouth twitched. "Ambulance," I whispered, squeezing the children. The pastor's face froze.

We lost track of time.

When the medical personal walked out of the bedroom their faces looked like dead stones. Victor tailed behind

"Victor," Bill and I didn't really know how to ask.

"Guys," the man didn't know how to express it. Bill and I looked at each other. The poor girl clung to me, assuming the worst. A second of her father's silence stretched into eternity. I knew his wife faced eternity. Was she ready? Just last night she was partying and bragging about her kids studying the Bible. "Not for me," she said then. Where was she now?

"Victor," Bill whispered. "Victor, how is she?"

Bill knew he asked a silly question. But what else could he, an American guest, do in this foreign country lacking so many life conveniences and necessities?

"My wife . . ." Victor began crying. "Yulia, my wife . . . Guys, she's . . ." The man began sobbing. "My wife. Thank you. For praying. She is fine."

I looked at Bill. I was overwhelmed. Yet, I was happy that these children hadn't lost their mama!

But their mama had to be careful. She was ordered to stay in bed. Only later in the evening could I see her. She looked exhausted even then!

"Yulia, I'm so thankful," she said as soon as I came into her bedroom. "God brought you and Bill to us." Her voice trembled. "Thank you for praying. Victor told me. It happened, while I was cooking. I just didn't feel well. My heart . . . The last thing I remember was seeing my kids and Victor. I couldn't even say good-bye to them."

"What did the doctor say?"

"January 1 is not a day for dying." The hostess squeezed a shy smile. I suppressed my tears of joy—I still struggled to believe she was alive.

"It's amazing the ambulance came. Everyone said it was God's miracle," she proclaimed. "Yulia, it's not safe to be in this world without God." The woman's eyes looked deep.

"No, it's not," I agreed.

"But then how could Victor and I brag about living without God? It's foolish!"

"Now you know."

"Could I accept Jesus?"

I couldn't believe what I had just heard. I got speechless. I became totally awestruck, for again and again I had witnessed how God answers our prayers.

He answers them even when they are clumsy or immature. He answers even beyond what we ask.He answers for He loves all of us. And that's the way God is.

RESCUING DOG-DOG

Rose Renee Wirth

"Where's Dog-Dog? There he is!" my grandson squealed. Who would think an old, worn stuffed animal could mean so much to a child? His oldest sister had given the fluffy, black stuffed dog to him when he was just an infant. Other children carried blankies, but Johnny had his Dog-Dog.

The day I rescued Dog-Dog I didn't realize that this little stuffed animal would be the only familiar face my 18-month-old grandson would see for more than a month. My oldest daughter was living an addictive and destructive lifestyle so she lost the privilege of being with her children. Although I have adopted one grandchild and had custody of two others at different times, in the case of my then-youngest grandchild, I felt I had to do the "tough love" thing.

"Honey, you know I love you but if you go back to using drugs after you have this baby, I will not take him," I had told my daughter months earlier. "Your destructive lifestyle hurts us all. Get help, go to 12-step meetings or whatever, but please don't jeopardize the baby by this cocaine addiction."

But that boundary was easier to say than to do. When the police department called, asking if I could pick up my grandson, I asked the officer if I could call her back, and I fell to my knees in prayer. The pain was so intense that I felt as if I were dying inside. If I kept my boundary, I surmised, perhaps my daughter would begin to accept responsibility for her life. Yet . . . .

"Oh, God, please help me to have your wisdom; I don't know what to do," I begged. "Should I step in again and rescue the situation, or will she learn more if I don't? Will she step up and be responsible for her son, if I back off? If I must step back, Jesus, help me. I don't know if I can endure the pain little Johnny is going through. I feel I am experiencing his pain and I can't get through this without your help."

I knew my grandson must feel bewildered and sad. I imagined him thinking, *Where's Mommy? Who are these people? Who will take care of me?*

Had I known then how long it would be before I was allowed to see baby Johnny again, I don't know if I could've kept the boundary I had given my daughter.

When I called back and talked to the officer about my dilemma and some of the circumstances, she seemed to understand.

"Ma'am, we're finding more and more of these cases where grandparents are shouldering the care of grandchildren," she said. "We're taking your daughter to jail for cocaine possession. You can contact the Department of Children and Families to see your grandson."

I had previously contacted a caseworker to check on Johnny, so I knew whom to call. By the time I connected with him, my daughter was in jail and Johnny was already at foster care. I was assured I could visit my grandson the next day. But that didn't happen. Every time I called I was put off with "tomorrow," a day that never seemed to come.

Frustrated, I prayed again, "Lord, please let Johnny be in a safe, loving home with a kind caretaker, and take care of him. Have your will in his life, I pray."

While I was thinking and praying about little Johnny I wondered if anyone who took him realized that his special stuffed dog was like a security blanket to him. I called the motel where my daughter had been staying when she was arrested and asked about the little black dog.

The kind desk clerk sent someone to check the room. "We have belongings that are being kept until your daughter pays her bill," she said after talking with the manager.

"Could you tell me if the toy I described is there?"

"Yes, it is."

I hurried to the motel, desperate to get something familiar into my grandbaby's hands. When I arrived at the motel and explained, the young desk clerk sent someone up to the room to bring Dog-Dog down. The tip I gave her was the best money I have ever spent. I rescued Dog-Dog for little Johnny. But since I still wasn't allowed to see him, what was I to do?

A few days later a sympathetic secretary at DCF took pity on me. She let me leave the stuffed animal at the office for Johnny.

Still not happy with the runaround I was getting, I decided to write a letter to the judge. I knew from previous experience that she was a wise woman.

Please, Lord, let me have Your mercy and help to be able to have contact with little Johnny.

The judge quickly let me know she would make a special visitation situation for me. I was grateful to be allowed one hour with Johnny and the foster mother before the court hearing.

One thing that had helped me during this month was that I was allowed to have e-mail correspondence with the foster mother. She seemed as happy as I was that a visit was arranged. Ava, Johnny's oldest sister, and Gabrielle, his young aunt went with me and we were thrilled that Johnny still remembered us. There he was with Dog-Dog! Even though I often wondered what his little mind thought about the situation, his overcoming spirit had taken over and he was just as happy as ever.

Later, the court would arrange for Johnny to go to a new home with his big brother who had been adopted previously. We visited the boys every week. It's been more than seven years since that sad time took place and Johnny is now a happy boy, always on the go, but usually not too far from Dog-Dog.

I know God heard me at one of the lowest points of my life and answered my prayers. My daughter, Johnny's birth mother, has successfully completed a stay in an intensive residential treatment facility and the Lord used my boundary with her to bring good for my grandson. Every time I see the delighted look on Johnny's face, I know that rescuing Dog-Dog was one of the best things I ever did for my grandson.

SURPRISED *by a* SOCKET WRENCH

Wayne Vanderpoel

Some folks carry a little cross to remind them of God's faithfulness; others have a picture of Jesus in their wallet. With me, it's a chromium-plated, 11/16-inch socket wrench.

The story began in a migrant workers camp in Florida. I had never seen one before and was in a state of shock. A little hollow-eyed girl, her bare feet brown from the raw sewage that rain had flushed from under her trailer home, peeked at us from around its rusted corner. I smiled and she ducked out of sight.

I looked at the other metal trailer shells sagging on the muddy morass and, shaking with emotion, clutched Pastor Bill Cruz's arm. "Are all the camps like this?" I asked.

He nodded solemnly. "Mostly. Some better, some worse." He had invited—more like dared—me to accompany him to a camp where he ministered. He felt God wanted me to see it.

Like most of the hundreds of such camps in Florida, this one was hidden away where the average person couldn't see it. Some three hundred thousand migrant workers—men, women, and children, practically all American citizens—work during the growing season from October through April; they follow the harvest of Florida citrus and vegetable crops in their cars, picking oranges, lettuce, tomatoes, and other foods.

Though some of them work for family farmers under good conditions, most exist at the mercy of labor contractors representing large corporate growers. Many of their shacks or trailers have no gas, electricity, or plumbing.

Pastor Cruz didn't need to say anything more. All I had to do was look. Weary fathers and mothers dragged themselves in from the fields, many leading children as young as two and three, who worked alongside them to make ends meet.

One of the men saw Pastor Cruz and his eyes lit up. He hurried over and extended a gnarled hand. "*Muchas gracias, Padre,* for the shoes and clothes for my *niños,*" he said.

After he left, Pastor Cruz said sadly, "We bring what we can, but it is never enough."

I knew why he had wanted me to come out here: to help. But I already had my plate full. I had a job rebuilding fire- and storm-damaged homes, and did a lot of church work, teaching several Sunday schools and doing other church projects. In addition, my wonderful wife, Marie, and I were taking care of my mother, who was ill.

But those migrants and their needs haunted me. I couldn't stop thinking about them. When my mother died, I thought the best thing I could do in her memory was to give my newfound time to the migrants.

I talked to local churches and temples, explaining the migrants' needs; people began to donate food, clothing, and toys, which I then distributed in the camps.

But something happened one Christmas day to confirm my resolve that this work was what God wanted me to do. Pastor Cruz called with an urgent need. "Wayne, we have sixty migrants just in from Georgia with no place to stay. We put them in an unheated building, and they have no blankets or sleeping bags. The temperature is falling to 18 degrees tonight. They'll freeze. Can you help?"

"I don't know," I said. "We just gave away all the supplies we had." Then I added, "But we'll pray about it."

Marie and I got on our knees and asked God to bring us the blankets. "Dear Lord, you know how much those people need them," we pleaded. "Please help us get them in time."

Then we went about our business. As Marie was fixing lunch, I said, "I know what I can do; it just came to me!"

I called up our local country music radio station. I got the disc jockey on the phone and told him we desperately needed blankets for people who would be sleeping in the cold. "We have to have them by tonight, sixty of them," I said. "Please put out an appeal asking folks to bring the blankets to my house. I'll get them to the migrants."

I figured I could use our church van, which was parked in our driveway over the holidays.

The deejay laughed. "Do you know what day this is?"

"Sure, Christmas. Why?"

"In the first place, nobody's even listening to the radio. They're all celebrating. Nobody will bring you anything."

"If you put out the call," I said, "God will handle the rest."

"Okay, guy," he said, laughing. "I'll play along with you." Right away I switched on his program. Ten or eleven songs passed without his saying anything. Finally, he told his listeners that blankets were needed for some people who were freezing, and gave my address as the place to take them.

Less than 15 minutes later a car pulled up in front of our house and a lady came up our walk holding a blanket. Another person brought two. Within a half hour, cars were lined down the street and around the corner.

"We'd better start getting the blankets in the van," Marie said. I began packing them. But the van was quickly filled to the ceiling—and we still had four piles of blankets in the yard. And cars continued to pull up.

"Marie," I asked desperately. "What are we going to do?"

"Take the seats out of the van, Wayne," she suggested.

I figured it would take an 11/16-inch socket wrench to unfasten the seat bolts. I went to my toolbox, but I didn't have such a wrench. Where could I get one today? All the stores were closed. And the neighbors were either gone or were busy with their own festivities.

So we did the only thing left to do. Marie and I went into our house, got down on our knees, and asked the Lord to provide the right tool.

But as the day waned and shadows began to lengthen, a thought nagged at me that maybe my faith was misplaced. I shrugged it aside and kept believing.

About five o'clock a lady drove up and walked down the driveway holding a small grocery bag. She said she had come after hearing the broadcast.

"I don't have a blanket, but here are some children's clothes," she said, thrusting the bag toward me.

I took it and, while thanking her, felt something hard in the bag. I looked in the bag—and pulled out a wrench, 11/16 of an inch to be exact.

I was stupefied. As the woman headed for her car, I called, "Ma'am, why did you put this wrench in the bag? It's the very thing we needed."

She looked puzzled. "What do you mean?"

"We asked for blankets but you brought this. Why?"

"I really don't know," she said. "I started out of the house, had to come through the garage, and saw it lying on my husband's workbench. He's been dead for four months and it was just where he left it. Migrants work on their cars, I thought. So I scooped it up."

"When did you leave?" I asked.

"About 45 minutes ago."

I looked at my watch. That was just when Marie and I were on our knees asking God for a wrench.

Within 15 minutes I had the seats unbolted and moved. As we drove out to the migrant camp that evening, blankets piled to the ceiling behind us, I knew I would give up my full-time insurance repair job and make this my life's work.

Today, our Migrant Care Ministries makes life a little easier for some one hundred and fifty thousand people throughout most of Florida every year. And when things get a little hectic, or the needs seem impossible to meet, all I have to do is look up at a chrome-plated 11/16-inch socket wrench mounted on my office wall.

TO PRAY *or* NOT TO PRAY

Betty J. Dalrymple

The three of us huddled beside the recently covered grave, tears freezing on our cheeks.

"You know what, Mom?" my older daughter asked. "I don't know if I believe in the power of prayer anymore. I mean, weren't all those prayers just a waste of time?"

"Wow, do I understand that feeling," my younger daughter agreed. "Hundreds of people were praying for Dad and he still died, I sometimes wonder, 'Didn't God hear all of our prayers?'"

Like a zombie, I stood there in shock and whispered, "At any given time, I often feel the same way." Then I asked the question that haunted me night and day, "How could this have happened? I felt sure our prayers would be answered and your father's cancer would go into remission."

As those days of shock and sadness dragged on, I often returned to that cold January morning's conversation. But how could I give up my belief in the power of prayer? After all, prayer was a priority in my life. My husband, Richard, and I always taught our children to pray. As an adult, I studied books on prayer, and when I read the story of the battle between Israel and Amalek in Exodus, I became fascinated with intercessory prayer. I learned that it was not only the fighters on the field of battle, but also the intercessors on the mountain that made a difference. I didn't want to bury my prayer life in that grave with Richard, but doubt became a monster that crept in during the night and chided, "Remember how hard you prayed and how sure you were that God would answer?"

Then I'd remember how I tried every possible way of praying. Maybe if I had said the right words in the right way that would help. Perhaps if I prayed on my knees, or visited the prayer room at church, that would make a difference.

Even if the doctors said there was no hope, I would not believe them. I could not imagine life without Richard and I knew God understood and would not let him die. I would not accept their prognosis because I believed in the power of prayer. I knew like those Israelites, our many prayers would help us win the battle for extra time together. The internal argument continued because I knew in my heart I could not live without God in my life and that meant including prayer in my daily schedule.

One morning as I wrestled with the prayer question, the phone rang and my friend asked, "Would you please pray for me? I just found out my breast cancer has returned."

I put aside my questions, stuffed my doubts, and said, "Of course I will."

I rejoined our prayer ministry team, prayed for family, friends, and many others. But something was missing. I had trouble focusing during prayer time, both at worship services and during my personal times of reflection.

As the cold winter days turned to springtime, my daughters and I continued visiting the gravesite. "How do you two feel about the power of prayer now?" I asked one morning.

"I'm still angry," my older daughter answered. "But I'm joining a prayer group at church. Maybe that will help my attitude."

"I'm trying to put some of those feelings away because they just cause me more pain," my younger daughter responded.

"I'm glad," I said, but inwardly I admitted, *Something is still missing in my own prayer life. That miserable cloud of doubt sneaks in and haunts my prayer time.*

"How's your spiritual life," a friend asked me one day as we met at a local coffee shop. This wasn't an unusual question because she and I often discussed our faith journeys.

I paused, then said, "I just feel like something is missing and I don't know what it is. Ever since Richard's death I feel like I'm lost in a forest of doubt and I don't like this feeling!"

"I'll pray for you," she offered.

Maybe God will listen to her, I thought.

This mental battle about whether to pray went on; however I continued participating in our prayer chain at church. Because of that, I often caught glimpses of God's grace and love. I wrapped those moments around me like a security blanket.

Finally, in a simple quiet moment, I heard God's voice and found my answer that chased away those nagging doubts. As I sat in my comfy rocker one morning reading my daily devotion, I read about a man who faced a scary situation and suddenly, he had a sense of peace. His first thought was, *My wife must be praying for me!*

Someone must be praying for me!

"I know how that feels," I whispered. "I've experienced that many times." Memories flashed through my mind—the time I had the breast biopsy and it was benign; when my father's prognosis was six months and he lived four more years; when we lost our family business and Richard was offered a good job at the right time.

And how many times had God shown me that He cared about the little things in my life? Like those times I'd prayed for my children's success in their school events; the God-incidences of a nudge when I'd lost something; or the perfectly timed loving words spoken by a friend.

I sat back in my rocker, closed my eyes, and whispered, "Thank you, God." In that still quiet moment, I heard God say, "You always believed, but your mind was sidetracked by anger, confusion, and disappointment."

The following Easter, when my daughters and I took spring flowers to the now grassy gravesite, we talked about good memories. We laughed at their father's humorous sayings and all the fun times we'd had as a family.

"Remember when we questioned prayer?" I asked.

"Yes, and I still don't understand why our prayers weren't answered as we wanted God to answer them," my daughter said.

"I don't either," I answered. "But recently God reminded me of many answered prayers from the past, including some since your father's death. Even though we don't understand why God didn't answer our big prayer the way we wanted, God loves us and wants us to continue talking to Him—and to keep believing prayer is the mightiest power on earth!"

"Amen!" they both agreed.

a BLOSSOM among THORNS

Betty Ost-Everley

"This is the last house we're looking at. Period."

As my husband parked our SUV in front of a brown, cedar-shingled ranch and waited for our realtor, I could tell that Terry wasn't kidding.

We had been looking at houses for more than a year. When we began, it seemed that "now" was a good time. Terry was handy, and we reasoned we could buy a fixer-upper. We were renting in a wonderful, upscale neighborhood, but our landlord was in frail health and we knew his family didn't want the houses. Our last child was leaving home for college and we really needed the tax break owning property would provide. Then in the middle of our house search, my mother had fallen and was recovering from a broken hip. She would need to be looked after more closely and would probably move in with us. All were good reasons to find a suitable house soon.

But after a year, our enthusiasm was waning. We had done all the homework we could up front, including becoming prequalified for a loan. But the process wasn't going just as swimmingly as we imagined. We now realized we wouldn't really get as much house as first thought, and probably not in the neighborhood we wanted. Looking at what seemed like one hundred houses, we had seen flips gone bad, foreclosures that had been robbed of anything even remotely resembling copper, and bullet slugs in walls, telling a story I didn't want to know.

"Fixer-upper" evidently was equated to "a hunk of junk."

So here we were at the absolutely last house we would tour. Both Terry and I had sought God's leading. Circumstances seemed to indicate we were doing the right thing, but what was God telling us?

The realtor arrived and opened the front door. A rose bush next to the porch welcomed us with its cheery coral-colored flowers. Inside were beautiful hardwood floors, generously sized rooms, and few steps for Mom to maneuver. The view out the back was a double-lot with shade trees and songbirds flying from one branch to another. It looked like a house in the woods, belying its urban address.

And the price was right. Well below the top-end of our price range, it seemed the house fit the bill. The area was racially integrated, which we liked. But the house was also on the wrong side of a main thoroughfare that was considered an income and cultural Mason-Dixon Line.

"This one might be the one, but we need to think and pray about it," I heard Terry tell the realtor.

More than he knew. I nodded. I liked the house, but I was hung up on its address.

A few days later, Terry concluded that God was telling him we should buy the place.

"Are you sure?" I queried. "I haven't heard that yet."

I usually made decisions quickly, but right now, I was the one on the fence. Maybe my fears about the neighborhood were not letting me clearly hear God's voice.

A few days passed, and without confirmation, I pushed away my concerns and signed the contract. A couple of months later, we moved to the new address, followed by the installation of our first security system, painting, and cleaning. We prepared to move my mother, and transferred our church membership to a neighborhood congregation.

Our first week in the new house, one of our dogs disappeared. That was odd since he was 15 years old and didn't exhibit any desire to venture outside our fenced yard.

The day we discovered Chance was gone, a couple of kids from the next block showed up at the door, demanding a reward for "finding" our dog.

"He wasn't lost. He disappeared from the yard," Terry stated.

"No, we found him. That means we get a reward. We want 35 dollars," they replied.

"First, I want to see where he got out."

The kids showed him a small hole in the fence, but Terry was not convinced that Chance had gotten through it on his own.

"Okay, come back this afternoon."

I was certain we were being played for fools, and I wasn't going to perpetuate the behavior by handing over money for a ruse. We purchased gift cards from a nearby fast food restaurant and gave them to the kids when they appeared, expecting their self-mandated reward. They grumbled with colorful language and obvious irritation . . . but the dog didn't disappear again.

We learned later that these children lived in a drug house.

Once more, I questioned God if this was indeed where He wanted us. Surely my husband had mistaken God's leading. This was an area filled with foreclosures and Section Eight housing, no grocery store, and few redeeming qualities. Some of my friends wouldn't visit because they told me they didn't think the area was safe. I was beginning to feel isolated. And God wasn't responding to my pleas for an answer.

The holiday season arrived, and we got to know more about our new neighborhood. I baked Christmas cookies to deliver to neighbors, which I had done for 15 years in my old area. Instead of gleeful acceptance, our new neighbors took the tins hesitantly, hiding behind partially opened doors.

Winter passed and transformed into spring. Spring meant neighborhood children rode their bikes up and down the street. While most of the bikes were in disrepair, having one was an important statement. As soon as the kids learned Terry had an air compressor and tools, our house was a frequent gathering place. Basketballs and tires were aired and bicycle chains were repaired. It was typical for Terry to help a group of six or eight kids work on bikes in our driveway, sometimes every night.

At these times, Terry was also able to have conversations about staying in school, getting good grades, the need to go to college to obtain a good job, and saying no to drugs.

During one bicycle-repairing session, a red-haired young man walked down the street, scrunching up his face and growling racial comments toward my husband.

"Why don't you stay with your own race?" He said, calling Terry a racist name.

We were shocked. We had never heard sentiments like that. Within the week, Terry had a T-shirt custom lettered, which he wore especially when working with the kids. "Old Crazy White Man" was on the back, with "I Luv My Hood" on the front.

We prayed for that young man. We knew he was the son of Paula, who lived across the street. One of the few residents who had welcomed us to the area when we moved in, her reception had cooled now that we were trying to revitalize the neighborhood association. In fact, we faced a lot of resistance getting the required signatures to reorganize the group.

"You'll never get anything done." "People around here don't care." And those were the words from the people who opened their doors. Most of them didn't. But we kept trying.

By the time we'd been in the house a year, things slowly started to change for the better. Our efforts to rebuild our neighborhood association were noticed. We reached out to the other two neighborhood associations in our area and began to meet monthly. Before long, other people and groups joined us, forming a coalition, and grass-roots efforts emerged to tackle some very large issues.

I was surprised as I saw Paula tentatively enter the coalition's monthly meetings. "I'm so glad to see you here, Paula," I said as she let me hug her.

"I heard that you guys were trying to get a grocery store."

"That's right. And our group is working on attracting an accessible health clinic."

"I was wrong about you and Terry. I'm sorry."

"That's all water under the bridge, Paula. We're just glad you're here."

Before the meeting was over, she signed our petition for our association reorganization and encouraged others to do the same. The next day her son apologized to Terry for his words. We had an ally and were getting support.

By then, my prayers had shifted from asking God if He had planted me in this place to asking what He wanted me to do. So far there had been no shortage of work, and, He was taking our group on a fast and fantastic ride. Our group was successful in keeping our community center open despite a huge budget shortfall in the city's budget.

We are currently applying for non-profit status and will find an operational partner to keep the community center serving residents. Neighborhood clean-ups are making the area more attractive and healthy. The health clinic is nearing a reality and is helping us attract a grocery store. God keeps bringing people with specific experiences and talents to work with us. I have no doubt that He has blessed our efforts.

My prayers were answered, just not in the way I expected. God was more interested in transforming lives than in what my address said to others. I was being shortsighted and not listening closely enough, putting God in a box. I didn't understand that His plans were so much larger and better than mine.

Just like the rose bush planted beside our front porch, we have found, and have tried to plant, His blossoms among thorns.

MANDY *and the* BLIZZARD

Ted Weaver

"The roads are not officially closed yet, but we strongly recommend no traffic. Snow drifts have covered the pavement and an additional ten to twelve inches are forecasted for tonight."

This word of warning came from State Troopers to describe the hundred-mile stretch of road between the West Texas cities of Lubbock and Sweetwater. But it was late in the day and we needed to go on home.

My daughter, Carole, her best friend, Mandy, and I had been part of a weekend arts and crafts show in Levelland, Texas, but the show was cancelled soon after lunch on Sunday due to heavy snows. We loaded our craft items and display tables in the pick-up and stopped by my parents' home in Levelland to say good-bye. Both girls needed to be in school Monday morning.

Mom and Dad agreed with the State Troopers' advice. "Don't go."

I was familiar with the stretch of road and decided to go anyway. Mom fixed us some sandwiches and sent a couple of blankets. She urged us to fill up with gasoline and drive carefully.

Soon after leaving, I could see that my decision had been a mistake. There was no traffic and for good reason—snow completely covered everything and was coming down so hard that we couldn't even see any tracks of previous traffic. I could only guess where the edge of the road was. We traveled slowly, pressing into the white wall of falling snow and the increasing snow drifts.

Our situation was serious. I asked the girls to join me in singing some hymns and choruses. These were familiar to Carole but not to Mandy. However the dangers around us soon had her picking up words and joining in.

Even as we sang, the pickup began to slide sideways, down an incline. We came to rest unhurt, facing the opposite direction and apparently well off the highway. The snow had so completely covered everything we were not sure where the road was.

The pickup engine died during the slide. This was serious. We had not hit any trees or guard rails and had not gone off into a gully or canyons. We sat there for a few minutes just to settle our nerves and to analyze what we needed to do.

The truck was getting cold so the logical first step was to restart the engine. I tried and only got a weak whirr as the battery was too low to start the engine. Our situation moved from serious to critical!

We were near the mid point of the hundred-mile stretch of highway that was surely now blocked to all traffic, with more snow piling on the significant amount that had already fallen. We were off the road, had a dead battery, and night was falling fast.

I began to sense the gravity of the situation. The wind chill must be near zero. We had some food and two blankets; not nearly enough for what might be hours or even days of isolation. Only my parents on one end of the road and my wife on the other knew we were on the road. They probably would not report us as missing for several hours. Also we were an unknown distance off the road.

I tried the starter again. Nothing! The girls silently looked at me. They were not yet teenagers and their futures might depend on what happened now.

"Girls, we need to pray." We held hands and simply asked God for His help. As with the songs, this was familiar to Carole but not to her unchurched friend. The critical nature of the situation made desperate measures realistic. Both girls prayed. By this time, we had lost heat in the pickup cab and were shivering.

"Dad, try to start it again."

I reached for the key, paused, and said, "Lord, we need you."

The engine turned over and started! All three of us began to weep and shout together.

"How could it start? The battery was dead," Mandy asked.

"Because we prayed," Carole replied. "God heard our prayers and answered them. God is real."

Mandy was wide-eyed. "This is unbelievable!"

The pickup was running but we were still off the road in sub zero conditions with heavy snow falling. Prayer time again.

"God, we need your help to get on the road and to get home," we told Him.

I left the truck to survey our situation but could see nothing except white. The road seemed to be uphill to our left. We would need somehow to turn around, climb the icy hill and find the road. Prayer time again.

Back in the cab, the heater was working. We thanked God for the engine and full tank of gas and again joined in prayer.

Mandy was a part of the process now as she said, "God, you can do it! You are awesome."

He did. We were soon back on the road but the conditions did not improve and we encountered no traffic. Our headlights revealed only white and so we prayed more as we slowly covered the last half of our trip.

"God can do all that!" Mandy stated as we neared home.

"Yes," said Carole. "And there is more. He loves you."

"Me, with my family mess and all that?"

"Yes, and he wants you to be His own." Carole told her friend about knowing God personally and led her in prayer to ask God to be part of Mandy's life.

We finally arrived in Sweetwater. The hundred-mile trip had taken more than eight hours. We were the only traffic on the road, but we were not alone!

FINALLY *with* HIS FATHER

Kelly Ruffcorn

His dark brown eyes and mischievous grin drew me to him. He liked to drive fast, shoot baskets and dance. Two years older than me, Randy carried himself with a confidence and an assurance that I did not possess.

At 15 years old, I was a shy bookworm whose favorite hobby was playing the viola in our city's youth orchestra. I had never loved anyone besides my relatives, never kissed anyone but my immediate family. I was studious, committed to church and family, and deeply devoted to my Lord Jesus.

Against my better judgment, I was drawn to this somewhat wild and rebellious youth, and he to me. We dated for a year, and I loved him as much as a young girl's heart can love.

Randy came from a broken home, with no father in his life. Although his mother deeply loved him, he desperately longed for the love and connection that only a father can bring.

I knew Randy's father was still alive, and I could not understand why he refused to be involved in his son's life. Before long, I realized Randy needed so much more than I could offer. I could see that he needed a father's guidance, friendship, and unconditional love.

I began to pray fervently for him: *Lord, Randy is lost without You. Please bring him to know You so he will spend eternity with You.*

I felt that God was calling Randy to His heart, and that I must share my faith with him. I pleaded for him to come to church with me, "Come on Randy! Just give my church a try."

"Oh, why not," he said with a smile. For the next six months, he attended church and youth group with my family. He became more and more excited to go each Sunday, and increasingly connected to our youth group leaders. Randy told his mother that he wanted to talk with someone about his father, his life, and about God. She found a counselor to meet with him.

The transformation of my sweetheart was astounding. He made better life choices, and longed to know more about God's love. He didn't tell me much about his counseling appointments. But I knew he was changed, and that when he was ready, we would rejoice together that he had given his life to God.

Our one-year dating anniversary neared and everything seemed perfect. Yet, even in the midst of this joyful time, I felt the longing to keep praying for him. I didn't know exactly why.

Then on a dreary Monday morning at the beginning of March, I pressed through the crowded hallways of my high school and plopped down on a worn wooden bench to wait for Randy to arrive. The last morning bell rang sharply as students filtered into their various homerooms. I began to wonder what would make him late that morning. Was he ill?

A few moments later, I stood and gathered up my books and bag. I had taken a few steps when I saw my mother walking toward me down the hall of my high school. What was she doing there? Why did she look so pale and alarmed? My mother pulled me toward the closest exit.

"Mom, what's the matter? Why are you here?" I questioned.

"Kelly," she whispered. "There's been a horrible accident."

Instinctively, I knew it was Randy. I also knew without her saying a word that he was dead.

My mother explained with anguish in her shaking voice that Randy had been in a car accident the night before. "There was a deer in the road. He over-corrected his car and rolled it several times on the highway." She clutched me, thanking God aloud that I had not been in the car with Randy.

"There must be some mistake, Momma. I just saw him yesterday and we were . . . . " My voice faded as we passed a sea of green lockers. My mother was pulling me through the parking lot to our family car as quickly as possible.

In the car she explained that Randy had been ejected from his car, landing on the pavement. A medical helicopter airlifted him to a nearby hospital, but Randy's injuries were too severe. He was declared brain-dead shortly after midnight, and moments later he stopped breathing. He died in Intensive Care. A petite respiratory therapist had pumped air into his lungs with a hand-held resuscitation bag while a tired nurse held his scraped hand. My young sweetheart, who was so full of life and exuberance just hours before, was gone.

In the days after Randy's death, grief nearly suffocated me. Violent nightmares made sleep terrifying for me. I curled into the fetal position between my parents at night. They said I was crying in my sleep. My dad's comforting words drifted into my subconscious, "I'm here, my Kelly. You'll make it through this. God has you and He has Randy. He loves you both very much."

I prayed for God's strength to go to the funeral home and view my beloved's body. I had never seen a body in a coffin. It seemed so wrong to be going for the death of a young person. I kept asking God, "Father, help! Why let me love him if you meant to take him away? Please show me that he is with you."

As I walked into the funeral home, I almost walked right back out the door. I did not feel strong enough to view his body, and the stale, chemical stench in the funeral home made me feel nauseated. I fought the urge to run and slid into a gilt and red velvet chair in the foyer. I mustered up enough strength to bow my head and whisper Psalm 86:6 – 7, "Hear my prayer, O Lord; listen to my cry for mercy. In the day of my trouble I will call to you, for you will answer me"

Within a few moments I looked up to see a frazzled woman walking through the front door. She knelt beside me as if she knew me. She reached up, grabbed my hands, and said, "You're Randy's girlfriend aren't you? Kelly, is it?"

How did this woman know me? I had never seen her before. "Do I know you?" I asked with confusion.

"No. Oh dear. You don't know me." She took a deep breath, "My name is Gordia. Oh maybe I shouldn't have come. I don't want to intrude, but I have something I have to tell you. Is Randy's mother here, too?"

I asked someone to find her while I eyed this woman as if she might be confusing me with someone else. Soon, Randy's mother joined me as Gordia began to explain to us that she had been Randy's respiratory therapist on the night he died.

She choked on her words and tears streamed down her cheeks. "I'd never believed in God before Randy was brought in to Intensive Care. I now know that God is real and that He loves Randy, and He loves me." She looked at us with a mixture of sadness for our loss and elation over her encounter with God.

She explained that as she was pumping breaths into Randy's lungs with the resuscitation bag, he spoke to her. Randy's mom and I felt shocked. How could a brain-dead person speak to anyone? Gordia explained that he spoke to her without using his voice. Only she could hear him. God spoke for Randy's spirit, and for several minutes she had an end of life conversation with my first love.

In her mind she saw a clear picture of Randy's mother and of me. That is how she knew my name and was able to come directly to me in a crowded foyer at the funeral home. She said Randy asked for her to tell his mother and Kelly that he was not afraid. Finally he would be with his Father. God was waiting to hold him, to love him, to know him as only a Father could. Randy had been waiting for this moment all his life.

"In all of the years that I've stood by a person's death bed, nothing like this has ever happened to me. I tried to forget what had happened," Gordia said, resting her tear stained face in her trembling hands. "I was so worried that you'd think I was crazy. I knew I wouldn't have a moment's rest though until I found you and told you all that I heard from Randy . . . and from God."

As she left, Gordia wrapped her arms around the two of us and whispered, "One more thing I almost forgot to tell you. Randy wants you to know that he'll always love you both, and that he'll be thinking of you from his home in heaven."

At that moment, I could almost see Randy's playful grin as he was enjoying the awesome gift of assurance that God had just given to his mother and me. For the first time in days, I smiled and felt relief, thankfulness, and joy. God had answered my prayers for a better life for Randy.

I now realized why I had prayed for Randy all these months. I found out from his counselor that he had received Christ as his personal Savior just a week before his accident. Randy told the counselor that he was drawn to me because there was something different about me—a light inside, a peace that he wanted. He realized after going to church with me, and meeting with his counselor, that the light and peace he saw in me was Jesus.

Much fruit came out of Randy going home to his Father. Not only did Gordia, Randy's respiratory therapist, come to know the love of God, but his funeral service was so God-centered that many of our high school friends gave their lives to Christ. Even Randy's mother became a strong Christian woman in the months following his car accident.

Twenty-three years have passed. I am now married to a precious man who loves God, our two beautiful children, and me. I am a teacher and have had the chance to tell my students how God faithfully answered my deepest prayers for Randy and for my future.

For me, the biggest fruit came in the great realization of God's goodness. I thank Him for the opportunity He gave me to share my faith with Randy and to know, beyond a shadow of a doubt, that Randy is forever with his Father. That is the hope that we can each hold on to until it is our appointed time to go home to our Father's waiting embrace.

the CRADLE *of* LIFE

Susan M. Watkins

Betrayed. By a young body designed to give life. She ran her hand across an abdomen quietly sheltering a seventh pregnancy. What would become of this conception? There was no excitement with the news. Fear greeted the ears of those involved. Six pregnancies. Two viable. Four spontaneous miscarriages. Empty cribs and folded clothes. Each time her body was weaker, from the constant fight against itself and her dreams.

I had often heard this story—mostly on warm summer nights as I stood behind my mother rubbing her shoulders or brushing her wavy blonde hair. We'd talk with the kitchen windows open, though they failed to release the inside heat or let the evening air enter. Shadows stretched across the wall, and streetlights illuminated our intimate conversation. From my position I could see where it had all happened years earlier. Mom still wept tenderly as she unfolded her formerly bruised heart before me.

I was older before knowing the whole story. Well into adulthood, I finally heard all. Gradually, I grew to understand the volatile scene behind that now visible door just off the kitchen.

At the time, God was a relative stranger to my family, known through ritual, not relationship. He was a "special occasion" God. But in crisis, somehow He became clearer and nearer.

Six pregnancies. Only months earlier, the last had produced my brother. He was perfect. Wanted desperately by all with two older sisters ahead in line. But my older brother left for heaven before tasting earth during his first trimester, and Mom delivered him alone. By herself. Behind that bathroom door.

He came prematurely, was baptized by her heartbroken unanswered tears, carefully swaddled, and carried away by my father to the doctor's office in a shoebox serving as his casket. Lifeless and never to be seen by us again this side of heaven.

Mom was sternly warned about subsequent pregnancies: There were to be no more. Ever. To allow one would surely take her life, now too weary to recover. Medically advised to stringently guard this occurrence, my parents took every precaution available for that decade.

But God is the Author of life. Months after my brother's departure, I was implanted in my mother's womb. For now, only two of us knew of my secret life: God and me. He kept me hidden in His secret pavilion while He formed my innermost parts.

Unbeknownst to me, a battle was waging and my tiny body engaged in warfare. What appeared to be a safe, protective environment was actually a battlefield with a life-to-death ratio against my favor.

As I quietly grew and clung to life, my mother discovered the unthinkable, and peace raced from her presence. Crisis, disguised as God, was at the door relentlessly knocking. There was no choice. It had to be answered.

With greater purpose in mind, the Lord answered Mom's early prayers. She and Dad were awash in fear. Still mourning the loss of my tiny brother, they now faced an even graver threat. Sleepless nights passed before the doctor's appointment arrived.

As a family friend, he, too, was anguished by news meant to bring joy. He had medically cared for my mother through four failed pregnancies and had a compassionate heart, but his advice created further conflict for my parents. It seemed that only one solution could spare my young mother's life. I was to be terminated. My life extinguished. No court, jury, or judge. A death sentence without opportunity for defense. A life for a life.

My father faced becoming a widower; my small sisters, becoming motherless. A legitimate funeral loomed on the horizon. Not the informal variety my miscarried siblings experienced. No. A casket, hearse, and grave, with my mother's voice permanently silenced. How could the few ounces of my tiny life outweigh that?

No one could hear me . . . but God.

Still unborn, I couldn't read the Almighty's Word penned by Isaiah, promising to carry me from the womb into old age. I could only trust the One who had placed me in my mother's body and planned my life before I drew my first breath or had my first thought.

For my parents, days and nights of fear and uncertainty melted together like crayons in a hot car. They turned the problem around and around. Though they'd never wanted a miscarriage, they now would have welcomed it so they could avert their personal decisions. But I tenaciously clung to her womb and fought the history and worn path of "spontaneous abortion."

The doctor urged them forward. My parents prayed to an unfamiliar God for guidance. He appeared silent. The deafening quiet of a still, steady God. It is here, at this seemingly uncaring and indifferent intersection that the deepest growth and trust are born in Him.

Again, the doctor summoned their decision. I was growing and time was against us. The decision for life or death was heavily upon them. If I was allowed to live, Mom would die. Being hinged to her own life, I, too, would die if she died. Inescapably, I was assigned death. With or without her. My life for her life. Her life for mine. The doctor called again.

With the framed Hippocratic Oath behind him, the doctor medically explained my appointment with death. It was not to be a back room abortion, but it was to be a much guarded pharmaceutical execution. A series of ingested pills would dislodge the "problem" and snuff my life. I would eventually go the way of my non-viable siblings.

My mother would feel discomfort, but she would survive and our family would remain intact. The emotional death she would suffer was never addressed. My parents decided to end my life in lieu of hers. There seemed no other solution. Tears and prayers appeared to fail and bring the opportune answer. I continued thriving and immediate steps were necessary.

My dad was to drive to the doctor's office and collect my lethal poison. Since he was unable to emotionally manage this journey alone, my maternal uncle offered assistance. I later learned he knew the ultimate destination. He was delivering the executioner to his pregnant sister and unknown niece; but was genuinely motivated out of love, concern, and the strong bond between them. They had spent their childhood defending each other through life's challenges, and this proved no different.

How perfectly formed were the pills that lined the bottom of that brown glass bottle! It mirrored my own physical perfection. I was not malformed or abnormal. My mother wasn't ill or fighting disease. Our nemesis was blood. There is life in the blood, only ours wasn't compatible. Her type was "negative." All offspring were "positive" like our father's type. This incompatibility caused the spontaneous miscarriages.

My dad and uncle returned home with the doctor's "treatment." They handed it to my mother, who disappeared behind the bathroom door showcasing a beautiful glass doorknob. A solid history of heartbreak was behind that door. Somehow the ornate doorknob camouflaged the reality. My dad and uncle played with my unaware sisters, not knowing what would transpire in that locked room.

God does His best work in our darkest hours. His light shines brightest there. Although some may not discover His light for years, God is patient and understanding. God Himself spoke everything seen and unseen into existence. Those involved in my situation were speaking death. My mother's and mine.

With water glass filled and pills in the palm of her trembling hand, Mom prayed a final prayer. Drowning in apprehension, she pleaded with heaven to honor the life it had given. Life's Author gave her the courage to act. Somehow God would make a way and protect life. Ours. A healing touch enveloped us. Mother and daughter cocooned. All the pills went down. Directly into the toilet. Mom refused to let her body become my grave, and she seized God's hand for safety in newfound trust.

At that moment, Passover visited her womb. The angel of death sharply flew away, seeing her sacrifice. Mom recognized she might die while carrying me, but perhaps I'd be developed enough to survive. God knew best and was invited to dwell in our family.

A father and mother's frightened prayers delivered an eight-pound, four-ounce miracle. I am alive today because my parents sought our loving God and chose to believe in the unseen. The Lord responded and came down to rescue His children. Reassuringly, He has known every one of us from the womb.

"Prayer is powerful." This is written across T-shirts, in greeting cards and books, on inspirational calendars, and in forwarded e-mails. Pastors preach it. Choirs sing it. For me, it's written in capital letters across the canvas of my life. The power of prayer isn't housed in the person who utters the words, but rather in the power of the One being prayed to!

The Lord secured my mother's womb. The faith of my parents' prayers made our blood compatible and Mom's pregnancy uneventful. We grew simultaneously. The doctor who'd advised them to end my life ultimately delivered it and I became his favorite patient. I am literally an aborted abortion.

Along life's journey I've had many opportunities to experience God's steadfast intervention. He has delivered me from afflictions and shown Himself true from the womb until my eventual old age. Still cupped in His capable hands, I am secure.

The Bible declares that the mouths of nursing infants will praise Him.

I am living proof.

in GOOD HANDS

Marvel Castro

I shifted in my seat in the medical van, feeling edgy and out of sorts. I was on my way to a dialysis treatment and had barely managed to get my kids, eight-year-old Shanequa and seven-year-old Corey, onto the school bus before the van arrived. I hadn't even had time for breakfast. And I always eat breakfast.

At the hospital I entered the dialysis unit. "Marvel, there's a phone call for you," said my nurse, Kim.

"Ms. Castro?" asked the voice on the other end.

"Yes," I said hesitantly as my mind raced, *Did Corey fall off the monkey bars? Is Shanequa feeling sick?*

"We have a kidney for you."

I sank onto a chair, my head spinning. *Is this real?*

For years I had been on a list to receive a kidney transplant. It had been so long since I'd been waiting that I'd about given up hope. So many times I'd heard those words in my dreams. Then I'd only to wake up and have to face yet another dialysis appointment. I'd been going for the treatments three times a week for eight years.

The woman continued, "We need you to come to University Hospital right after your treatment. There's no time to lose." Then she hung up.

At last there was hope! No more dialysis. No more feeling tired all the time. I would be able to look after Shanequa and Corey on my own. We'd moved to Syracuse from Rochester when I divorced my abusive husband. With no family in the area I had to call social-service agencies and leave my kids with strangers whenever complications from my illness landed me in the hospital.

Now for what I hoped would be the last time, I notified Exceptional Family Resources, an organization that places kids temporarily with families in its network. I had used them before. This time, I'd need two weeks to recover. Two weeks of my children being in the hands of strangers.

"Don't worry," Kim assured me as she hooked me up to the dialysis machine. I hardly felt the needles go in, I was so anxious.

"God, please send someone to take care of my babies," I prayed over and over as the machine whirred and the hours ticked away.

Afterward I was rushed to University Hospital and given a stack of papers to fill out. As I signed the last form, a phone call came for me.

"Marvel? My name is Debbi Hier. Your children are with me and they're fine."

"Let me talk to them, please," I said.

"Mama," Corey said. "Are you sick again?"

"No, Baby, I'm going to be all better now," I reassured my little boy.

"Are you coming back?" he asked. I winced at the doubt in his voice. *Does he think I'd leave him alone?*

"Of course, Corey. So you'd better behave yourself, hear?"

Then Shanequa mumbled hello. She gets quiet when she's scared. I could picture her big dark eyes peeking out shyly from behind her braids. Debbi came back on the line.

"I didn't have time to pack their clothes," I said. "Corey acts up when I'm not there . . . ."

"I'll take good care of them, Marvel. You just get well."

My doctor came in and I said a quick good-bye to Debbi.

"When's the last time you ate?" he asked, checking my pulse.

"I haven't had anything all day," I remembered.

"Good. Then we can operate today. The sooner the better."

The rest of the evening was filled with surgery preparations. Thoughts of Corey and Shanequa pushed everything else out of my mind—even the operation.

Please, Lord, I prayed as they wheeled me into surgery, *let this be the start of a better life.*

When I woke up the next morning I didn't feel any pain. I lay staring at the green zigzags skipping across the monitor. The kids would be getting ready for school by now.

What will she pack for their lunches? I wondered.

The doctor came in. "Everything went well," he said.

"When can I go home?" I asked.

"Slow down," he said. "You need a little recovery time."

I tried to rest, but couldn't stop thinking about the kids. They called that evening. "We're fine, Mama," said Shanequa. I was amazed at how strong she sounded. "Guess what? Debbi has two dogs—Brutus and Lady."

Dogs! Corey was terrified of dogs.

Then Corey called out from the background: "They're so much fun to play with, Mama. I wish you could see them. And Debbi gave us ham and pineapples for dinner!"

I felt a pang of hurt. Pineapples and ham? Imagine that! Sounded like special cuisine to me! Who was this woman?

Debbi got on the line. "Their routine won't change, except I'll pick them up and bring them here after school."

She sounded so confident. And why not? She probably had a big house and enough money to spend on special dinners every night. How could she possibly know how hard it was to raise kids on your own?

"They're doing fine, Marvel. My two girls love the company. You just concentrate on getting well. Don't worry about a thing."

Easy for her to say, I thought. *I bet she never had to turn her kids over to strangers.*

Then a new worry gripped me: What if the kids liked staying with Debbi too much? I knew it was silly, but they hadn't even asked when I was coming back!

The next couple of evenings the kids had more stories about Debbi's house. I listened patiently, told them to eat well and be good, and hung up with hardly a word to Debbi. The happier the kids sounded, the more miserable I felt.

"Lord, what's wrong with me?" I asked.

I lay in bed one afternoon, my mind drifting back to all the nights I had stayed up worrying about how I would put food on the table for the kids, how I would manage to buy them new clothes for school. Now some other woman was dressing them. *She doesn't even know who I am, where I've come from . . . .*

A nurse came into the room. "You have a visitor," she said. "Debbi Hier."

I grabbed the mirror off the bedside table and smoothed my hair. I sat up straight in bed, trying to look as strong as possible.

Debbi walked in, and my eyes immediately focused on her blond hair, falling in neat curls to her shoulders. Then I looked at the rest of her. She was full-figured like me, not tall and slender and intimidating as I'd imagined. Her face had a softness that caught me off guard.

"Hello, Marvel," she said, squeezing my hand.

"My kids okay?"

"Yes, they're fine. They're at school. Since they're not allowed to visit, I thought I'd come see how you were doing."

I motioned to the chair near my bed, eyeing her warily.

"You look different than I thought you would," I said.

She smiled and handed me get-well cards the kids had made. "The first day they were so down I could hardly get them to talk," she said.

I looked her in the eye. "I know you probably take in lots of kids whose parents don't want them," I said. "But Corey and Shanequa aren't like that. They have a home."

"I know that, Marvel." Her sincerity was unmistakable.

At the end of the week I was released. I couldn't wait to show the kids their new, healthy mama—one who would always be there, whose arms would never be too tired to hold them. But they would have to stay with Debbi for one more week while I recovered at home.

The night before the kids returned, I set to cleaning house. Everything had to be just right. I wanted Debbi to see what a good mom I was. I kept picturing her reaction, how she would look at me in my home with my kids and not find one flaw. The next morning I was too nervous to eat or drink anything. I kept pacing in front of the kitchen window, checking the clock.

Then I saw them coming. I threw open the door and Corey and Shanequa bounded up the steps. "Hi, Marvel," said Debbi from behind them. I wrapped my arms around my babies, letting them wipe away my tears.

"Shanequa, Honey, what happened to your hair?" It was pulled up in a ponytail.

"I'm sorry, Marvel," Debbi said, flustered. "I let the braids out to shampoo her hair and I didn't know how to get it back the way it was. How in the world do you manage to do all those little braids?"

"It's okay," I said. "I'll fix it later."

"I'm sorry," she said again.

Some quality in her voice struck me. It was like a bridge across the gap between us. I looked in her eyes. They didn't have the look of judgment I expected, but instead the same insecurity I had seen in my own in the mirror that morning. *She seems nervous too!*

"Please sit down, Debbi," I said, pointing to a chair at the kitchen table. Gently, I pulled away from the kids, kissed them both on the forehead, and sent them upstairs to play.

"I was afraid you wouldn't like the way I did things," Debbi began, then looked down.

I felt a rush of warmth toward her. "I was a nervous wreck about the kids coming back," I confessed. "They seemed so . . . happy with you."

"All I tried to do was distract them from how much they missed their mommy," she said. "They're great kids. My daughters and I will miss them. I was wondering how you would feel if maybe they came to visit sometime?"

I had promised myself never to give my children to anyone else again. Yet for the first time I saw what my kids must have seen in Debbi. She was not a stranger, but a friend God had sent to comfort and love them when they needed it most.

"I think they'd like that," I said, covering her hand with mine. "Maybe I could show you how to braid Shanequa's hair."

"Really? That would be wonderful, Marvel."

"But only if you promise to fix pineapples and ham."

WHERE HAVE THEY TAKEN LORRAINE?

Wallace Wanlund

A scream shattered the late afternoon stillness. I was in the garage, removing the bumper from our car.

"Wallace, they've got Lorraine!" my wife, Vivian, yelled from the front lawn.

I ran into the street thinking maybe dogs had attacked Lorraine, our lovely, blonde, petite 17-year-old daughter. Vivian was running toward an orange van parked across the street. I raced past her asking, "What happened?"

"He has her purse."

Lorraine must be on the other side of the van, I thought. A tall, dark man was climbing into the van on the driver's side. I grabbed him, trying to pull him out of the vehicle. I was at a tremendous disadvantage; the driver high up in the seat, and I, standing on the street. We grappled.

"Get the gun, Billy! Get the gun!" the man screamed.

A hand holding a gun came around the doorjamb, and stopped inches from my head.

This is it, I thought. There was a deadly click.

Misfired? Unloaded?

I was distracted long enough for the driver to break my hold. The van moved. I tumbled backward. I grabbed at the door, but let go as my wife yelled, "I'm getting their license number."

The van gained speed–my heart went with it.

Lorraine is in that van.

Vivian ran toward the house, repeating the license number. I waited to see which way they would turn on the highway. Then I raced toward my car. "I'll follow them; you call the police."

I reached in my pocket. No keys. A frantic search. A desperate cry to the Lord. I finally found them on the garage floor. The key in the ignition brought only a buzz. The safety belt lockout. I buckled the belt and squealed out of the driveway.

They were gone!

I couldn't believe it had happened. Our quiet neighborhood, with nice homes overlooking the Pacific Ocean, had little excitement. Now, our daughter had been kidnapped in daylight.

As I drove toward home I called desperately upon the Lord, "I commit Lorraine to You–only You can help her."

I turned onto our street and police cars seemed to be everywhere. A command post was established in our home. A police officer advised me, "We've covered the neighborhood for any information the neighbors might have. Officers have been alerted. Freeway entrances and exits are being checked, along with beaches, parks, docks and hills. CBers have the license number and vehicle description. A helicopter has been dispatched."

He looked at me a moment, then added, "The orange van was stolen about an hour ago. We've been advised that the men are armed and dangerous."

"Just what happened?" another officer asked.

"Lorraine was waiting for a friend to pick her up," Vivian said. "I glanced out the window when I heard the van stop. I saw her point down the street, so assumed she was giving directions. I turned away, but looked back to see the driver clamp his hand over her mouth, grab her purse, pull her behind the van. She screamed and I ran out."

One of our neighbors, the organist at our church, came into the room. "I'm calling Father Harry and asking him to get the prayer chain going right away."

"I'm also going to call my mother," I said. Mother, now eighty years old, had been ordained a minister at age 78. She was a life-long Bible scholar. We needed her strength, prayer, and faith.

"Lorraine has been kidnapped," I explained to her. "She needs your prayers."

Through the two phone calls to Father Harry and my mom, in minutes an amazing prayer net was spread across the county that involved several hundred people. Prayer chains called other prayer chains and prayer groups. Some groups were in session when the calls came in. They called others. The prayer chains crisscrossed, the prayer net covering far more area than the police dragnet ever could.

We pushed aside thoughts of what could be happening to Lorraine, and placed our confidence in the Lord.

What was happening to Lorraine was this: Her abductor shoved her into the back of the van, and began tearing her clothes. She fought and cried. Suddenly the driver yelled, "Cut it out, Billy."

"What do you mean?"

The driver picked up a tire iron from the front seat and threatened, "Cut it out, or I'll break your legs!"

The prayer net had begun to tighten.

They argued until they became violent. Lorraine was glad it took their minds off her. They seemed to be driving in circles, apparently not knowing how to get on the freeway.

"Come here and see what's in her purse," the driver ordered.

"I'm going to tie her up first." Billy took tape and bound her hands, ankles, and mouth. Just before he taped her eyes shut, she saw a sign—they had found the freeway entrance. Lorraine's spirits drooped. On Southern California's intricate freeway system she could be miles from home in minutes. She wriggled in protest. Her captor slapped her face.

They entered the swiftly moving traffic. Lorraine lay huddled in the back of the van, a prayer in her heart.

Then they heard a sound that brought hope to Lorraine, while it carried terror to her abductors.

The steady chopping of a low-flying helicopter.

The men panicked. "That's a Fuzz-copter. Her ma got our license. They'll get us for sure. We got to dump this chick."

The prayer net tightened.

They swung off the freeway. Blindfolded and gagged, Lorraine had no idea of where she was or how long she had been in the van. Her one thought: *What are they going to do with me?*

The van stopped. The side door slid open. They lifted her, carried her a few feet. She held her breath. Then those violent men, who had been well prepared with a stolen vehicle, binding tape, a lethal weapon, and deadly purpose, set her down gently in something soft. They drove away.

Lorraine lay motionless a few moments, then began working at the tape on her mouth. She was bound with her hands in front of her, but releasing herself still took time. When her mouth was free she struggled to get the tape off her eyes. She looked around.

She was lying in an alley on a pile of sawdust and wood shavings behind a carpenter shop.

"Help! Help me!" she called.

Three men ran out, their faces showing their amazement.

"I was kidnapped!"

They untaped her wrists and ankles, and got her to a phone.

The prayer net had closed around her—tight, secure.

She dialed . . . .

My phone rang at exactly 6:10 PM—only one hour and 15 minutes after Lorraine had been kidnapped. A police officer answered and handed me the phone.

"Come and get me," Lorraine sobbed.

Relief swept through me. "Are you all right? Where are you?"

"I'm okay, Dad." She gave the address, about 15 miles away.

Two uniformed officers went to pick her up. I wanted to go, but they told me to wait at home with my wife.

Vivian and I held each other closely, praising the Lord.

About an hour later Lorraine ran into my arms. Home! Safe!

Her long, blond hair was full of sawdust and wood chips, her face tear-stained. Our daughter is a very shy, private person, and we realized it would be difficult for her to talk about her experience. The policemen realized it, too, and were very considerate of her feelings.

One asked, "Do you want to go to the hospital?"

"No, I wasn't molested," she said. "He only slapped me."

She walked toward the stairs. "I'm going to bed. I'm upset and exhausted, but I'm all right."

Lorraine climbed in bed, wood chips and sawdust still in her hair, and soon dropped off into a deep sleep.

The policemen had been aware of our calmness in this crisis situation, and of our prayer activity. As they finished their reports, one man said thoughtfully, "The noise of the helicopter probably had a lot to do with them getting rid of her so quickly—they didn't know that the helicopter, and our officers, never saw them. But you know . . ." he paused and said with a smile, "Maybe it wasn't helicopter noise—maybe it was angels' wings."

The stolen van was later located, but Lorraine's abductors were never caught. They escaped the police dragnet, but they couldn't escape the prayer net!

a TRUE FRIEND

Shawnelle Eliason

I started praying before we moved. I'm a heart person, and I knew I'd need a gut-level friend—the kind who knows your heart but loves you anyway. I figured I'd get a jumpstart and ask early. After many months in our new home, I wondered why God still hadn't answered.

My three boys and I were sprawled over an old, patchwork quilt. The June sun steeped through our T-shirts and toasted our skin with summer.

"Do you like butter?" asked my toddler as he thrust a fistful of dandelions under my chin.

"Oh yes," I said. "But I like you more." I tickled his belly and he giggled.

I delighted in his hearty laughter. I hadn't laughed in a long time. I was lonely. The loneliness crept into every part of my day. We'd only moved 32 miles, but I regretted every single one. I missed my friends.

"What's the matter, Mom?" ten-year-old Logan asked me, noticing the expression on my face.

"Yeah, Mama. What's wrong?" parroted Grant, his seven-year-old brother.

I looked at them and smiled. My boys peered straight into my soul no matter how hard I tried to camouflage it.

"I'm just fine," I said. "Want to throw the Frisbee?" But I wasn't honest. My heart was heavy with hurt. I marveled that I could be lonely when I never had a moment alone. I was the mother of three little boys.

Our old neighborhood had been hard to leave. It was as near to Mayberry as you could get, and I'd grown accustomed to that lifestyle. Friends dropped in and joined the hum of our home without missing a beat. When we decided to move closer to my husband's work, I assumed that God would replace the blessing.

Lord, set aside a friend for me in our new community. A friend of your choosing. You already know who it will be.

My prayer was steadfast.

In our new home, the days were long. Without the connection to another woman, I felt lost.

I decided to be proactive. No more waiting for my doorbell to ring. The library seemed to be the hub of the community, and I signed the boys' names on any activity sheet that was offered. We'd troll for friendship.

One afternoon we ventured out to build log cabins made of milk cartons and twiggy pretzel sticks. As we climbed the stairs to the library's activity room, I was hopeful. Voices twined down the stairwell and I was eager to join the chatter. My boys squeezed my hands. They wanted to belong, too.

The room was a buzz of activity. Moms, kids, and pretzels were everywhere. I scanned the room for an empty seat and saw our neighbor. She nodded but didn't offer a place at her table. She was busy with her own friends.

"Where will we sit, Mom?" asked Grant.

I squeezed his hand. "I don't know, but we'll find a place," I said, as I wondered again how I could feel lonely in a crowd.

That evening, my husband, Lonny, and I spoke in hushed whispers before we fell asleep. "Are you doing okay, Shawnelle?" he asked.

Nighttime is my heart's on-valve. Words poured into the darkness.

"Lonny, it's tough. My old friends are busy. Sure we can visit, but it's not the same as living next door. I have no new friends. I'm lonely. My prayer for friendship hasn't been answered."

"How is your quiet time with God?" he asked.

I rolled into the down pillow to face Lonny. "That's the only thing that's been good since the move. God is speaking to me through His Word. It's like the words have come to life, or as if He is whispering in my ear."

"What is He telling you?"

"That He loves me. That He is faithful. That He promises to never leave."

"Yes," he said.

Lonny's arms circled me. I breathed deep and settled in.

During the days when I felt lonely, I called my grandfather. My grandparents had always been an anchor in my life; a constant source of encouragement and love for me. After Mamo went to heaven, Papo provided encouragement enough for both of them.

I called him frequently.

"Papo, are you sure this will work out?" I'd asked. "I don't do well on my own, and friends in this place are scarce." I bit my lip to ward off the tears.

"You'll be fine, Baby Girl. God is with you there," he said. His words brought the same comfort as they had when I was a little girl. Only I wasn't little, and it didn't take long for the loneliness to cradle me again.

"Will you pray for me, Papo? That God will send a friend?" I knew he would pray. And I pumped up my own prayers, too.

Lord, it's a simple request. Just one friend. I've never been so lonely. My old friends are busy and this new community is tough. I trust that You'll provide.

The days rolled on and the loneliness settled deeper. I began to feel angry. God continued to talk to me about His faithfulness, yet I remained friendless. I'd never had trouble making friends before.

What are You doing, Lord? Why aren't you answering?

I decided keeping busy would crowd the loneliness from my soul. The boys and I took walks, went to the park, and started to paint. We painted every room in our house. We painted until Lonny got home at night and peeled the roller from my hand.

I prayed as I rolled miles on the walls. One afternoon, as I pushed primer across the dining room, the phone rang. I plunked the roller in the tray, wiped my hands on Lonny's old plaid shirt, and rushed to answer. Mom was calling. Papo was sick. "You'd better come," she said.

Before long Papo joined Mamo in heaven.

The loss of my grandfather compounded the loneliness. Grief cocooned the ache and I wondered if it would ever go away. I sat at Papo's funeral and wondered how to exist without his encouragement. I hurt for the loss. And I hurt because God let him die right then, when I needed him.

I don't understand, God! I asked for a friend, and You've taken Papo away.

I sat on the straight-back bench, next to my husband and sons. Hurt bubbled from my heart. Then it pushed through my shoulders in deep sobs. I ran my fingers along my skirt hem and tried to pull the grief back in.

Lonny squeezed my hand.

When the organ began to play, I didn't pay much attention, though the melody was familiar and that brought some comfort. I'd heard it many times, a song called, "In The Garden."

Looking at my grieving family hurt my heart, so I closed my eyes. And as I sat with my hand pressed into Lonny's, my eyes squeezed shut, and my heart bruised, a strange thing happened.

God opened my ears.

The words of the hymn fell to my heart as if I'd never heard them before. "I come to the garden alone," the soloist sang.

"I know about feeling alone," I whispered. I opened my eyes. As I listened to the words, I saw beyond the slumped shoulders and broken hearts of my parents and sisters. I saw beyond my own hurt and grief. And I saw beyond an unanswered prayer.

"And He walks with me, and He talks with me. And He tells me I am His own," rang the chorus.

I remember Your Word, Lord. You love me. You're faithful. You promised to never leave.

"And the joy we share as we tarry there, no other has ever known." I couldn't believe my ears. God was offering me friendship. Plain and simple. He offered to talk, to listen, to spend time with me, to make sure I knew that I belonged.

And in that friendship, there would be joy.

"How can you offer this?" I whispered to Him. I felt ashamed. My eyes turned to the wooden planks on the floor. "I've been so angry."

"It's what you asked for," came His words. "A friend who knows your heart and loves you."

Lonny's arm draped around me. I breathed deeply and knew I would be okay. I'd met my True Friend.

As the months swept by, God did provide a sweet bevy of friendships with other women. But He brought this only after He'd revealed Himself to me in a new way.

He'd heard my prayers for a friend.

And He knew who it would be—all along.

a PRAYER *with* FLYING COLORS

Donald E. Phillips

I was going blank! Yet my future was at stake. I wasn't used to test-taking anxiety. Whatever you call it, it was a huge memory lapse, at the worst possible time. I thought I was going to forget all the Hebrew language I had learned. I stared at the test materials I was to translate. Nothing came to mind regarding their meaning or how I could translate them. I couldn't believe that was happening! I'd worked so very hard to be prepared.

Years of study toward a Ph.D. in communication studies were at stake. If I passed this exam of translating biblical Hebrew, I could reasonably expect to earn my degree and have a career in communication. If not, about five years of hard work would have largely been down the drain.

It was unusual that I was able to use Biblical Classical Hebrew as my "language tool" for my doctoral degree program. Most doctoral candidates at the University of Oklahoma used German, French, Spanish, or statistics.

I felt God had gone to bat for me, answering my prayers to get my doctoral committee to approve my request to use Hebrew.

If I couldn't deliver on that request I would be extremely embarrassed. Likely, my faculty advisor and department would be, too.

To fail this exam, even worse, to be unable to translate it at all, would have been a complete disaster. Another graduate student in my department had failed his exam and it put him back in his program quite a ways. For some, it could be the end of the line, with much of the "blood, sweat, and tears" of a demanding doctoral program wasted.

For several terrifying minutes I felt I was going to do worse than badly. I couldn't even think of any Hebrew! I faced being totally humiliated and set back. Probably, it would be the end of all my hard work in this program—about seven years' worth. This included my Master's, all my degree course work, and work on a dissertation, which I had started.

This wasn't just any test. It was a critical checkpoint in my degree program, to be followed later by 16 hours of exams over the field of communication studies, which I took over four days, followed later by a final oral exam of up to three hours, examined by five professors on my committee, including one from the philosophy department where I also studied theology. Finances, future, and respect were all at stake. If I ever had to pass a test this was such a time. I was playing for all the marbles. Unfortunately, for several horrifying minutes I seemed to have forgotten how to play the game.

I was locked in a carrel, a narrow, cell-like little study or test-taking room. All alone, in that little room, I was suddenly terrified by the sense that I could remember nothing of Hebrew even though I had studied it for three years to the intermediate level, and had reviewed for this exam for months—well, really, for years. I took a hard year of Hebrew in seminary, where we had a challenging professor. One student, quite bright overall, reported saying to the seminary Hebrew professor, "I don't know all these answers but God knows all of them." The professor replied, "God gets an A; you still get a failing grade."

After seminary I partly set Hebrew aside since I was involved in different ministries. But when I attended the University of Oklahoma to study communication and philosophical theology, I needed a language research "tool." The doctoral committee's agreement to allow this seemed a miracle. Rare. To get up to speed on Hebrew again and add to my knowledge of it, I took a review course in Hebrew under a very distinguished Hebrew scholar, Dr. William J. Horwitz, an expert in Ancient Near Eastern Languages. He was also a rabbi.

About forty Jewish students were in my Hebrew class. Once, before a hard exam, during a review in class, one student said "Dr. Horwitz, if you give us an exam as tough as that some of us won't be back next semester."

The rabbi replied promptly, "That's all right; the remnant shall be pure."

I was the one Gentile in the class. This resulted in very interesting discussions as I talked about the meaning of some Old Testament passages with the students and professor outside of class. I found my own faith strengthened. With a degree from Harvard and two from Yale, Dr. Horwitz was deeply knowledgeable of Hebrew, the Old Testament, and Middle Eastern culture. I discovered that distinguished awards are given in his name at Yale. So I was learning from an expert in Hebrew language who was also a renowned expert in Ancient Near Eastern languages.

How could I let him down, too? And all the others I would have to face?

As I looked at the test paper again, I stopped to pray in that little carrel. I gave my blankness and potential panic to God. I waited on God in prayer briefly. I stayed seemingly calm but keenly aware of all I had at stake.

An incredible change occurred. While several minutes before I looked at Hebrew passages and couldn't do anything with them, suddenly the answers all started coming to me. I translated the passages quickly. I felt I was in a different zone, with God with me.

I sensed God was with me as I translated all of the passages. I had been told my language exam would be taken from at least three Bible books: Exodus, Joshua, and Jonah, but I didn't know which ones would be used in the exam. I would have to know my Hebrew to a high level to get it right. I had prepared for all that, translating these books in my studies, carrying around language study cards, and putting Hebrew grammar and vocabulary on tapes. I remember being in Nashville with my family and they wanted me to get into the swimming pool with them but I declined because, I said, "I have to study my Hebrew."

We swam together other times but those were types of sacrifices I had made to learn Hebrew. Now it was sink or swim in this test and, with God's help, though it seemed I started out about to sink, I was now "swimming."

God, giver of every good and perfect gift, including the marvelous gift of languages, human and divine, intervened in that study carrel, empowering me to complete the exam successfully. Dr. Horwitz' official note about this exam, sent to the chairman of my committee, was, "Today Don took his Hebrew exam and passed it with flying colors."

I still have my copy of that document, inspiring me to continue to trust God and earnest prayer made to Him. We need to do our parts in facing life's tests. When we do we can also prayerfully trust God to empower us to successfully face and do what we need to do—an especially encouraging assurance at critical times of our lives.

God's incredible ability to answer heartfelt prayer (and headfelt prayer) can be the difference between sinking in life's tests or passing through them with flying colors.

LEAVE HOME EMPTY, COME HOME FULL

Nairy Ohanian

One morning during my first year on the mission field in Armenia, I was in one of my "Woe is me, I'm single" moods.

Armenia, after the dissolution of the Soviet Union, was a small, newly emerging nation with many challenges. I was one of the first foreign workers to live and teach there. It was December, it was cold, and I faced a constant battle to keep the apartment warm. I only had a kerosene heater, similar to what campers use, so during winter, I felt like I was on a never-ending camping trip.

I stared at my bread, cheese, and tomato breakfast pondering my situation. *Where will I find kerosene? How can I store enough for the winter? Why doesn't anyone help me? I am sick of doing these tasks all by myself. Why don't I have a husband to help me? Every woman my age in Armenia has a husband. Why did I come here as a Miss?*

By the end of breakfast, I was puzzled as to which I really wanted more, a husband or heat.

I knew prayer was my only hope and comfort. As I spent time in genuine, though chilled, prayer, I returned my focus upon the Lord and trusted Him to make my kerosene hunt a success.

I left my apartment with two empty plastic containers and a hopeful heart. I started my winter wanderings by going to all the nearby gas stations. *Station* may be a generous word for a man sitting next to a gas truck, waiting to funnel fuel into your gas tank. I asked each man if he had kerosene or knew where I could purchase some. After a few blocks, I found a man who actually had a gasoline pump and not just a truck.

"Do you know where I can find kerosene?" I asked. He stared at me and then promised to find some for me. He instructed me to leave my containers with him and return in twenty minutes.

Wait, this sounds too easy. Should I trust him with my containers? What if he does not return with them?

I really had no other options. I left the station and decided to visit one of our ministry staff members who worked in a store nearby. I visited with him for about 45 minutes, as I knew most Armenians were usually relaxed about time. I figured my fuel man could not have possibly returned in twenty minutes from his kerosene source.

As I approached the gas station nearly an hour after my first appearance, the gas station man exclaimed, "You are forty minutes late! Where were you? Didn't I say twenty minutes?"

Beside him stood two full containers of kerosene. He did it!

"Where do you live?" he asked me. I said I lived about six blocks away, but could carry the containers home by myself.

He insisted, "Jump into my car. I will take you there."

What? I did not know this man. However, he was trustworthy with my containers and impressively punctual. I quickly calculated the extra money he would charge for a ride since many people used their cars as taxis. I just shrugged and figured that the clever man had figured a way to make a little more money. I decided to splurge and save myself a strenuous walk home. He loaded the kerosene into his trunk, opened my door, and away we went.

"What are you doing here?" he asked while he drove.

"I serve as an English teacher and as the Director of the Christian student fellowship in the city," I replied.

"But why would you come to Armenia? Everyone is trying to leave this country," he continued. I told him I was convinced that God had led me here and that I wanted to encourage students by bringing them hope in a difficult time. He was surprised by my response.

"But where is your family? Your husband?" he inquired.

Funny you ask, I thought, *as I was just wondering that myself.*

I informed him that my husband was yet to be found, but that I had a wonderful family back home.

He finally understood and said, "No wonder you have to fill the kerosene."

I learned that in Armenia, specific tasks are designated for either men or women. Evidently, I was doing a man's task. Later, I discovered that most men will quickly help when they notice a woman doing a "man's job." They figure if a woman is doing such a task, she has no brother, father, or husband, and therefore other men are socially obligated to assist her.

We arrived at my apartment building and he promptly jumped out and lifted the kerosene containers from the trunk.

"Which floor do you live on?" he asked, kerosene in hand. What service, and right to my door! But I said, "No problem, I can really handle it from here."

"How much do I owe you?" I asked, while computing the kerosene and taxi costs in my head.

"Nothing," he quickly replied.

"You can't pay for my kerosene. How much?" I insisted.

"You're helping our people; that is plenty. Just come by whenever you need anything." He disappeared into his car and swiftly drove off.

I stood with two kerosene containers full, but my mouth empty of words.

What had just happened? I was ready to be cheated, but there I stood not having paid a dime. These things weren't supposed to work out so smoothly. I felt convicted. I had constantly questioned this man's character and motive, imagining theft or kidnapping! Had I not prayed to God and asked for His assistance in the midst of my singleness blues and the "manly" task at hand?

Not only did God answer upon my asking, but I also received so much more than I ever would have imagined: free kerosene, a ride home, and a new friend ready to help when needed.

Thank you, Lord, for caring for me whether I am single, shivering cold, or culturally clueless.

LOSING CONTROL *in the* SUPERMARKET

Kitty Chappell

"Lord, I feel so useless since moving here," I prayed, sighing. "I know it takes time to make new friends, find a church, and get established in a new community, but could you please speed things up a little?"

This had been my daily prayer since my husband, Jerry, and I had left a busy lifestyle in Southern California and moved to this beautiful mountain town near the Western Sierras. Jerry commuted to his business several hours away, and he came home only on weekends. So my days and nights seemed even longer.

"It's just until the business sells," he promised.

In our previous church I had taught Sunday school, had sung in the choir, and had mentored younger women. I was always busy—and I enjoyed feeling needed.

Now my heart ached, not so much from loneliness but more from a feeling of emptiness. I felt unfulfilled and just generally restless in my spirit when I was not busily involved in helping and praying for others.

After another pleading session with God one morning, I poured a cup of coffee and gazed out our huge picture window. Dark clouds hovered over the lush green valley while patches of bright sunlight shined through intermittently. Lightning flashed above the snow-covered mountains on the far side.

I mentally took stock of my kitchen supplies thinking it wise to go to the store before the winter storm hit. But I didn't really need anything. Checking the refrigerator, I noted the milk was low, but we had enough for several days. With rain imminent, I saw no urgency to rush out for only a gallon of milk. However, I was soon driving down the windy mountain road into town.

While fumbling for change in the supermarket, I heard a feminine voice ask, "May I carry this out for you?"

Not even in good weather would I allow that—a carry-out for only one item? It seemed strange that someone would offer.

Then something even stranger happened. Fully intending to say "No, thank you," I replied, "Yes, thank you."

Why did I say that? I wondered, as the box girl scooped up the milk. *When we get to the door I'll tell her I'll carry it myself,* I decided. But as I followed her through the door, my mouth remained shut. It was as though I'd lost control.

I puzzled over this as we walked to the car at the far end of the crowded parking lot. A light mist began to fall and I noted the smell of moist dust. Again in control, I said, "I'm so sorry to bring you this distance for only a gallon of milk."

"That's okay," she said. "It's my last carry-out for the morning. I'm going home."

"Great!" I said, placing the milk in the car.

"I'm only working half a day today, but it's really been a long morning—my first day back from a two month's leave of absence," she offered without expression.

I turned and, for the first time, looked at her. I'd not seen her in the store before but that didn't mean anything since we were new in town. She appeared to be in her late teens. Soft brown hair framed her pale pretty face, but her blue eyes were dull and lifeless.

"Have you been sick?"

She hesitated. "No, I was . . . raped."

"I'm so sorry," I said.

Without emotion, she related her experience. "I still can't believe it. I was only 18 and a virgin."

She had exited a store at dusk while shopping in a neighboring town where she lived with her parents. As she walked toward her car, she was suddenly grabbed and pulled behind a building where she was sexually assaulted at knifepoint. Her attacker warned her to tell no one.

After she had driven home, her mother had taken her to the police station where she endured the unpleasant process of reporting a rape.

Suddenly I understood what had happened in the supermarket. God had taken control so He could answer my prayer.

"Mary," I said, noting her name badge. "I understand some of your feelings. I was a teenager when my father, after years of abuse, almost murdered my mother and was sent to prison. But because I'm a Christian, God helped me to overcome my painful experiences. He can also help you."

She stared blankly. "I'm a Christian, too," she said sadly. "I was when it happened."

My heart flinched. I suspected her greatest pain was the feeling of abandonment by the One whom she had trusted the most, God.

"Mary, God loves you dearly. You are unique and special to Him. However, as Christians we have no free pass from pain. What happened to you is not uncommon in this flawed world, but it is not something God planned or wanted to happen. The good news is, as His children, we have access to God's grace and power. He can help us overcome anything. In your heart you must know this, Mary."

She nodded, but I wondered if she was ready to fully embrace that truth emotionally.

"God does not want you to be emotionally crippled–to feel you have no value, to trust no one, and to harbor hate for your attacker. He can help you to become even stronger and more compassionate. Because of your terrible experience you will find you are able to help others."

"Maybe He's using me already," she said, gazing at the snow-covered mountains.

"What do you mean?"

"Because I went to the police, they found and arrested my attacker. He's only 19, but has already assaulted nine women. No one came forward until I did."

"You are to be commended, Mary. Because of your courage perhaps many women were spared your fate or even being killed.

"I've thought about that."

"Your attacker is very troubled. He was stopped early in life because of your brave actions. Let's pray he receives help and allows God to change him."

Large, cold raindrops had begun to fall, but we didn't notice.

"Mary, your pain is fresh, but a time will come when you can address the issue of forgiveness. Only the strong can forgive. The weak, who don't forgive, remain in emotional bondage. I enjoy freedom because I forgave the one who wronged me. I can encourage you now because I am free."

We parted with a hug and my promise to pray for this precious young woman.

Driving home I shivered—not so much from my wet clothes but from the memory of her haunted eyes. "Please, dear God, help this sweet girl to heal and become whole again in You." This became my daily prayer.

Although I feared I might miss Mary in our large supermarket, she always found me. She magically appeared at my checkout stand to carry my groceries. We used every opportunity to talk. With each trip to the store, I noted more expression in her face and voice. I continued to pray. It felt good to be personally involved again with someone who needed me.

Several months later, Mary rushed up, hugged me, and whirled me around and around in the aisle.

"Guess what? I did it!" she cried out.

I'd never seen her so animated. Her eyes danced, full of light.

"You did what?"

"I forgave him—I really did! I feel so free!"

Though our meetings were limited to supermarket visits and occasional telephone conversations, Mary continued to share her life with me. She eventually began dating, fell in love, married a handsome Christian man, became pregnant, and then stopped working.

Just before my husband and I moved out of state, Mary called, wanting me to see her new baby.

We lived in that area for only three-and-a-half years, but my memories of Mary will last a lifetime—memories that were made possible when God took control in the supermarket and answered my prayer.

HE WILL TEACH YOU HOW *to* PRAY

Katherine Valentine

Nothing is lovelier than our beloved Connecticut in the fall unless it's Martha's Vineyard, which has the added feature of being surrounded by water. It's pure magic to stand on a high point surrounded by a wreath of brilliant golds and ambers to watch a flotilla of ships sailing in the distance, their masts reflecting the azure blue waters. Enchanting!

My husband, Paul, and I had returned time and again to the island that had a way of melting away stress. It was just the right backdrop for a long weekend of R & R.

The last six months had been difficult as Paul recuperated from a serious fall on a construction job. With no health insurance and few resources to pay the mounting medical bills, we had sold our home and cashed in what was left of our savings. After twenty years of marriage, we were starting again.

Although we knew this short trip would stretch our budget to the limits, we both felt we desperately needed it. And true to form, the island's beauty and tranquility recharged our flagging spirits. The only glitch in an otherwise perfect holiday was the need for a spot on the ferry that would take us back to the mainland. The only promise the ferry line ever made was to get you off the island within 24 hours.

We joined the endless line of cars snaking back and forth through the parking lot and settled in for a long, long wait. By 11 o'clock, the rays of the warm morning sun streaming through the windshield, coupled with boredom, lulled me into a gentle sleep and I began to dream.

I was facing a wall of silvery mist as a pair of huge male figures stepped forward. Although they certainly didn't look like any angels I would have imagined, I knew without a doubt that they were celestial beings.

They stood about nine feet tall and were dressed in long white tunics that sparkled as though covered in diamonds. As they advanced, I shrank back and knew why, throughout the Bible, angelic visitations often elicited fear. Their upper arms were like ham shanks, and I could see thick, corded muscles rippling just below their skin.

I was frozen both in fear and awe that I was actually standing in the presence of God's messengers when they walked behind me, picked up my legs, and carried me into the mist.

Moments later, I awoke as I heard the car engine being turned on. The ferry had just docked and we were finally on our way home. As Paul handed the attendant our boarding pass, I told him about the dream.

"At least they were angels, not demons," he joked, as he steered the car up the boat ramp.

Since it was a Sunday afternoon, the traffic was backed up from the Cape to the Connecticut border. It was a little after seven that night before I saw the familiar country lanes leading to our home. Paul pulled into the driveway when I noticed our daughter's car parked by the house. Heather was in her early twenties and rarely visited us. My first thought was disappointment that I hadn't known she was coming. I would have gladly cut our holiday short to spend time with her.

"I'll unpack if you'll start supper," Paul said, opening his car door. Knowing our daughter didn't like to cook, he added with a smile, "Or maybe, Heather has decided to surprise us with a home cooked meal."

I laughed and headed toward the house.

"Heather," I called, dropping my carry-on by the door.

"In here, Mom," she called from the kitchen.

"Hi, honey. What a lovely surpr—" I stopped midsentence.

Her eyes were swollen from crying. A bolt of fear coursed through my chest.

"What is it?"

She came around the counter and threw herself into my arms. "Oh, Mom. I'm so glad you're finally here."

"What is it, Honey? What's wrong?"

"There's no good way to tell you," she said. "Marissa is dead."

"Marissa? Dead?" How could our son's daughter, our three-year-old granddaughter be dead? *I must have heard her wrong!*

"It happened around 11 this morning," she began.

Eleven? That was the same time I had dreamed of the angels.

With tears streaming down her face, she explained that while our son, Daniel, was resurfacing his driveway, he had backed up a dump truck filled with gravel and Marissa had run out behind it. She was instantly killed.

"I tried to get you at the bed-and-breakfast where you were staying, but they said you had already left," Heather explained. "You have to get over there fast. They need you and Dad."

I raced back outside, my mind still unable to process what I had been told. How could my dear, sweet granddaughter be dead? And how could my son ever live with the guilt from the horrendous accident?

Suitcases were stacked beside the car. I shouted to Paul to put them back.

"Why?" he said. "I just took them out."

I repeated what Heather had told me. We grabbed each other and let the tears come freely. Finally, Paul opened the passenger side door for me to slip in.

"We'd better get going," he said, taking charge of his grief.

"You drive, I'll pray," I told him as we began the 45-minute trip to our son's house.

As I watched the familiar landscape rush past, I tried to filter through the enormous pain and settle on a prayer, but where should I begin? How should I pray? For peace? Comfort? Freedom from guilt? I cried out to the Lord: *Help me, help me! I don't know how to pray.*

Then I remembered the scripture in Luke that spoke about those times we were to give our thoughts over to the Holy Spirit for He would teach us what to say.

I bowed my head, fighting against the grief that threatened to lock my thoughts on the tragedy. Right now, our son and his family needed the support that could only come through intercessory prayer. Having no strength of my own, I humbly asked the Holy Spirit to pray through me.

What happened next could only have been the intercession of the Holy Spirit for I would never have prayed as I then did.

For the entire length of the ride, a spiritual battle raged as I heard myself praying with a force that was not my own. The Holy Spirit was commanding the powers of darkness to return to the bowels of hell as a fight raged on for our son's soul.

I had never prayed like this before, and the words that tumbled from my lips frightened me. Several times, Paul glanced over with a raised eyebrow. But I had asked the Holy Spirit to intercede with words that I was unable to find, and He had responded. Even though they were far removed from what I would have prayed, I decided to trust His leading.

When we arrived at Daniel's home, our son and daughter-in-law had the glazed look of those who are in deep shock. Paul and I gathered them in our arms, and only then, did we give in fully to our grief. No words were said, only the deep, mournful wails of unimaginable pain from the depths of our very souls for the tragic loss of a beloved, gentle spirit.

Around four in the morning, our son finally fell into an exhausted sleep. My daughter-in-law and I snuck into the kitchen to make a pot of tea.

While we waited for the kettle to boil, she turned to me with a new stream of tears staining her ashen face.

"Oh, Mom," she began. "I was so scared. About twenty minutes before you arrived, Daniel locked himself in our bedroom with a loaded gun. He said he couldn't stand the pain and wanted to end it."

I had no way of knowing this, but the Holy Spirit had seen the battle raging for our son's soul and had stepped in as his defense. I know without reserve that the Holy Spirit's intercession saved my son that day from taking his life.

Today, our son is a pastor. He and his wife counsel parents who have lost children. When I look back, I can see why Satan waged a war for Daniel's soul and why the Holy Spirit stepped in with such power. He knew our son would one day help dozens of grieving parents find the strength to go on, who might otherwise have lost their faith during one of life's hardest trails.

QUICKSAND!

Jim Ness

I had never met her, but her death in 1988 was never far from my mind: Adeana Dickison, young and on her honeymoon, hopelessly trapped in muddy quicksand as the incoming Alaskan tide closed over her head.

For hours, 14 men—including her husband—had desperately tried to free her from the silt's cement-like grip as the tide rose. During that time, those of us too far away to help kept in touch with the tragedy through our rescue communication network. But despite all efforts, nothing could save her.

Alaskan quicksand, which is as deceptive as it is deadly, can be found in coastal areas. Mud that is often firm enough to walk on may become a treacherous trap as the tide rises. Inland, similar dangers lurk under stable-looking peat moss.

This gray glacial silt is formed of grains as fine as talcum powder. If your foot sinks in it, the water flows out and the grains lock around your leg, pulling with as much as five hundred pounds of suction. The more you wriggle, the more you sink. Once a person is trapped, there's not a whole lot of hope for him or her. One victim was torn in half by a helicopter attempting to lift him from the tenacious muck.

The tragedy of Adeana's death touched many in Alaska, where church services were held all across the state in her memory. So I was not surprised when Bob Hancock, a member of our Alaska Mat-Su Borough Dive Rescue Team, called me one evening. "Jim," he said in a voice filled with emotion, "we've got to figure out a way to save people trapped in that stuff."

I heartily agreed, and under Bob's leadership we devoted countless hours to a mission that eventually consumed our whole group's attention. Even my wife, Pamela, a police officer and deputy chief of our team, along with our young son and daughter, joined in.

Whenever I could spare time from my plumbing business, I was in our garage working on ideas. Nothing seemed promising until Bob came up with the idea of using a long steel pipe jammed into the mud near the victim's foot to break the suction. Even better, we thought, why not a hollow pipe with a flared perforated end through which air could be pumped?

We tested this device on the muddy coastal flats of Cook Inlet, outside Anchorage. Under carefully created conditions, a team member played victim, with his legs in the mud. Others surrounded him so he could be pulled out if the device failed. They were supported on plastic foam Boogie boards. Using these—on which rescuers could kneel, stand, or swim—was Bob's idea. As we watched with anticipation, air was forced down the pipe. But other than sloshing up some bubbles, it had no effect.

Again and again we tried new ideas, consulting with many engineers, but nothing worked. There had to be an answer; why couldn't we find it? Then the thought struck me–I hadn't asked God about this. So I prayed, believing that when you work with your mind open to God's presence, illumination comes.

Then one morning I stopped at a gas station to fill a low tire on my van. As I pressed the hissing hose against the air valve, I realized the air we had been pumping through the pipe wasn't powerful enough. Why not blast highly pressurized air from a scuba diver's tank down the pipe? The operator could use a screw valve to control the air effectively.

Our team felt this might be the answer. But it was going to take time to develop. Anxiety took over until someone said, "Let's create with patience–and let God handle the impatience."

Trusting God to help us reach our goal, we decided to deal with the problem gradually until we had come up with the best lifesaving tool possible.

By early 1994 we were ready to test a new compressed-air pipe we thought would work. On a blustery spring day our team, drenched in icy salt water, labored on a volunteer up to his thighs in gurgling mud, under carefully controlled conditions.

"Deeper," I shouted to the pipe handler. "Get it under his foot. Feel your way." But the trapped foot wouldn't budge. Mud had clogged the air holes at the pipe's flared end. We returned to solid ground disheartened. That night I prayed desperately for an answer.

As I lay in bed staring up into the darkness it came to me: Drill the holes farther up the pipe.

I had no idea how this could help. But we decided to try it anyway. We welded shut the bottom holes and drilled five in the shape of a T about an inch and a half up from the flared end. In tests, the modified pipe appeared promising, and by May we felt that our mud rescue tool was as good as we could get it. A blast of air broke the suction for a short interval, allowing the victim's foot to rise a few inches. We speculated that a succession of airbursts would do it for a person who was almost entirely submerged. But until a real-life accident occurred, we wouldn't know for sure.

Our moment of truth came with an emergency call on the afternoon of June 15. Kris Armstrong, a 43-year-old carpenter, had been riding his four-wheel all-terrain vehicle on a desolate trail in the foothills of the Talkeetna Mountains. His partner followed on another machine. Neither realized that the wet spot ahead in the moss-covered trail was a death trap.

When Kris's vehicle hit the mud hole, it lurched forward, throwing him into the muck, which immediately began dragging him down. His partner tossed him a rope and attempted to winch him out. But as the rope became taut, Kris screamed in pain, "Stop—you're tearing me apart!"

His partner raced down the mountain and returned with two men. They eased a large inner tube around Kris and worked to free him. But the mud gripped Kris fast. Sinking deeper, he writhed in agony from the fruitless pulling that had already dislocated an ankle and torn knee ligaments.

A 911 call brought our rescue team to his side. Four of us—Archie Vasquez, Dave Laba, Ed McCain, and I—tumbled from our trucks with our mud rescue tool. It was a shock seeing Kris, pale and sunken up to his armpits.

Trying to keep my voice reassuring, I called, "We'll get you out, buddy. Just hold on."

You helped us create this device, dear Lord, I prayed. *I surrender everything to You—my hopes, dreams, and career. Just let the tool work!*

I shouted directions to the men positioned on the Boogie boards around Kris. Archie calmly and methodically worked the pipe down into the mud, all the way to Kris's feet.

"Dave, get the support strap ready. Someone else hold a Boogie board against Kris's back." Kris's mouth moved but no sound came. By now he had been immersed for six hours. We had to work fast. Archie squeezed the hose valve from the scuba tank, blasting 125 pounds of air into the mud beneath Kris. Nothing happened. When we pulled at Kris's arms, he stuck fast, as if encased in cement.

Oh, please, God, let it work.

Another burst of air. This time, as we tugged at Kris's body, we felt some movement. His right foot had lifted a few inches!

We were thrilled. But the mud quickly renewed its deadly grip. Again Archie let loose a blast from the tank. Foul-smelling air bubbled from the brownish-gray mud as we pulled again. Kris was moving!

Gradually, with burst after burst of air, Kris's body rose. One foot came out, then the other! Strong arms lifted Kris's mud-soaked body onto a stretcher. The rescue had taken only ten minutes. *Thank You, God!*

An exhausted but grateful Kris was rushed to the hospital, and we washed the mud from our new lifesaving tool. One life had been saved. And others would be.

VEIL *of* FEAR

Mary Kay Moody

I bounced along in the car's back seat, staring at the sky, a gentle shade of blue. As we rounded a sharp turn I fell against the window, then felt the horrifying sensation of the car sliding across ice. I gasped.

"Mom, relax!"

My son, Karl, was driving and resented my fear. He said he was learning to gauge the intensity of my whimpers and gasps to know if he must slow down, or if I'd just prefer he did.

I didn't respond. Mountains, bridges, flying—all these things torment me, and that irritates him.

The trip didn't begin this way. I'd grinned in anticipation as we drove Highway 89 north from Squaw Valley, then west into high country above Donner Lake. My husband, Ed, and I were visiting Karl, who loves wilderness—the more remote, the better. He wanted to show us some lost-in-time havens in the Sierra Nevada Mountains. So we climbed into his car and started up a cracked macadam road. I savored the view of jutting snow-capped peaks, their ruggedness softened by evergreens and lacy aspens. These God-given gifts refreshed my soul, which was wearied by the strain of my work with trauma victims. Vacations are to re-charge; this one had accomplished its purpose. Until now.

We ascended in ever-sharper turns, skated across gravel, and then bounced across a rock-studded dirt track. I didn't need to look at my hands to know my knuckles were white. I could barely swallow. I forced myself to breathe and looked at the sky instead of the road and scenery dropping before us. And I talked to God.

"Wooo-hoo! Isn't this great, Dad?"

I gasped again as we entered a tunnel.

"Wait," I rasped. No one heard. "Stop!"

"What?" The car barely slowed.

"Stop. Now."

Karl groaned. "Mom, we'll be there just past the tunnel."

The car rolled to a stop.

Ed patted my hand. "It's just a tunnel, Honey. Thought you'd prefer that to looking into valleys."

"How long before we get there?" I inhaled deeply, hoping I could endure.

"Twenty minutes. Maybe 15," Karl added quickly.

I shook my head and opened the door. "I'm sorry. I can't."

"What are you doing?" Ed asked.

I looked at him thinking he couldn't really miss that I was escaping the car.

"I want to walk."

I stepped out and spoke through the open door. "I'm better on solid ground. You guys go on."

"No."

"Please. I love walking through the woods. Maybe I'll catch up to you." I closed the door. "I'll be fine—as long as I can walk."

"I won't leave you alone out here."

Usually I appreciate my husband's protective urges. But now I wished he'd let me walk. I didn't want to ruin their fun, but to me it was torture. I just wanted to walk, enjoy the beauty, and let my racing heart and flipping stomach settle.

"Karl knows this area. I won't be attacked by a bear. And you know I won't get too close to a cliff."

"C'mon, Dad. She's right."

Ed shook his head. "I won't leave her. Turn around."

"Why let her ruin everything?"

"Karl!"

We headed back. The luster of the day, the reunion with our son, and my communion with God—ruined.

The next morning at breakfast I convinced the two adventurers to embark on the journey of yesterday and leave me at the hotel. It didn't take too much urging. I enjoyed watching their sparks of anticipation. Ed seemed to lose years in body and spirit whenever he shared wilderness jaunts with Karl. So I grinned as I waved them off in Karl's weathered pick-up.

Back in the lodge I grabbed my Bible and settled against the bed pillows. After reading I begged God to take away my fear. I reminded him that years ago I, too, had an adventurous spirit, and asked why my fear of heights had grown so great. Why He allowed it to steal the joy of celebrating with Karl, and reveling in His glorious mountains.

Most of all, I begged God to remove it because of its impact on my son. "Karl scopes out exciting places to share with us, but my fear shuts that down. He gets frustrated, cranky; we're all disappointed. And, Lord—what of my example? We try to teach him to pray, seek Your will, and rely on You. My fear must shout: 'Your mother tells you to trust God, but she doesn't do it.'"

I was truly puzzled, because I didn't plan on being afraid. I didn't even think I needed to be afraid. But terrors sprang unbidden from my body. Explanations made sense, but when the land fell away my equilibrium fell with it, and panic flooded my soul.

I finished my prayer, then hopped in the car to drive around Lake Tahoe. The beauty of this sapphire jewel soothed me; I explored piers, beaches, campgrounds, and overlooks. Every stop showed me a new facet of the stunning lake and its island.

Later the guys returned and told me about their adventures off-roading through abandoned railroad tunnels. Ed's face glowed. "We came out of an avalanche shed. I leaned out the window, glanced down, and saw no road! Looked straight into the valley."

They describe glistening Donner Lake, and feeling like adventurers as they stood above another tunnel, peered over the edge, and felt a shudder as the train chugged through and emerged below them.

"So, Mom, tomorrow we ride the Funitel up to the Gold Coast. You going?"

He had described that area atop the ski lift, an alpine bowl ringed by peaks that couldn't be seen from here, a mere 6,200 feet elevation. He worked up there amid dozens of ski lifts and restaurants. I wanted to see his territory. But riding thousands of feet high in a car dangling from cables?

"I want to," I said.

He tilted his head. "Really?"

"I'll plan on it, but reserve the right to change my mind in the morning." I almost said, "Chicken out."

He shook his head with a half smile.

"And if I do change my mind, you will go without me. I'll be safe, but sad."

The next morning, dressed in winter coats, we crossed the parking lot and entered the huge, shadowy building that housed the European ski lift, The Funitel.

Karl grinned and looked at me. "You ready?"

God, my Rock and Fortress, please help me. I can't get out halfway up and walk. Standing on solid ground is really the only way I enjoy mountain peaks and valleys. But I didn't want to miss this opportunity to connect with my son. He lived at the top of this mountain. If he wasn't working, he was snowboarding it.

I took a deep breath and nodded.

Karl beamed and slapped his leg. "All right." He sauntered to the waiting car, almost a small bus, and hopped in. Ed followed. I gulped and stepped in, too.

Within moments machinery whined and clattered. The car slid away from the platform and glided through the open bay door into the dazzling outdoors. The gondola swayed in the wind. I clutched the pole in the center of the car.

We seemed to be flying. I prayed as I looked at craggy granite poking through the snow, and watched the ground fall away. My stomach churned.

Ooops. Sky, Mary. I looked up, but it didn't help. The car's motion emphasized that I was in the sky, not on solid ground. I looked forward at the mountain face it appeared we'd crash into. That didn't help either.

"Look, Dad."

"Wow. What a sight."

Karl pointed out the side window. I peeked to the valley, hundreds of feet below. I rocked back and slammed into a seat.

"No, Mom. Out there."

"In a minute." I took a few deep breaths. Then I turned, avoiding a downward glance, and peering toward the horizon where he pointed. The deep peacock blue of Lake Tahoe glittered between mountain peaks.

Breathtaking.

I stared. I slowly realized that looking far away, I didn't sense I was hundreds of feet in the air. What a stunning sight—totally inaccessible from ground level. *Thank you, Lord.*

I began to relax and enjoy the trip. Suddenly the car shuddered. We moved from one set of sheave wheels, over the lift tower, onto another set of wheels. I clung to the pole again

"There are hundreds of safeguards, Mom."

"I remember." But at the moment, information didn't help.

The ride smoothed. It lasted only seven or eight minutes, and though it seemed like hours of endurance, it also passed too quickly. We reached the top, and chicken-mom happily exited the car.

We stepped into a winter wonderland. The snow, much deeper at 8,200 feet, was pristine. No footprint marred the glistening blanket. No ski track sliced through it. The snow sparkled in the mid-day sun. The only sounds: the whisper of wind through the pines, birds chirping, and our murmurs of awe.

I am profoundly grateful to have shared this view with my husband and son. Many years later it is still the image that instantly transports me to utter tranquility when I try to sleep after a jangling workday. Having the serene place to ourselves was a gift I'm convinced God gave in answer to my anguished prayer. And that would have been more than enough. But he gave my frightened heart an even bigger gift.

That evening Karl complimented me on my courage. I explained I hadn't felt courageous, just desperate; and I didn't want to portray a lack of trust in God.

"Mom, I never doubted you trusted God. When you were afraid it just felt like you didn't trust me."

Oh, the ache. How could he think that? Wilderness survival, tracking, first aid, mountain climbing, and ice climbing are just a few of the things Karl has studied extensively. There's no one I'd trust more in the outdoors.

"I'm so sorry, Karl. It isn't you I don't trust. In fact, it isn't about trust; it's about my body reacting to heights."

"Well, thanks for trying the lift. It feels really good to know you believe me."

Thank You, Lord. In Your amazing way of accomplishing many things at once, You removed my veil of fear plus rewarded me with glimpses of stunning beauty and of my son's heart.

the MIDNIGHT PRAYER

Bob Haslam

Grandma Wakeman sat up in bed suddenly out of a deep sleep in the middle of the night. There in Michigan, she experienced an overwhelming urge to pray for me, her former pastor, at that time a missionary far away in the Philippines. She knelt by her bed and interceded earnestly.

Mrs. Wakeman was Grandma to everyone around her. Wife of a retired pastor, she was a gifted and godly woman. Her spiritual gifts and the fruit of the Spirit in her life enabled her to counsel and encourage many believers in our congregation. She was a natural spiritual leader to all who knew her, and she was a consistent intercessor.

When I left for missionary service in the Philippines, she promised to be a faithful prayer partner. For three years she had kept my family in her prayers. We kept her informed of our situations and prayer needs so she could pray more effectively on our behalf. But I had neglected to tell her my true situation.

Now suddenly awakened, Grandma wondered what crisis might be occurring in her former pastor's life. She later told me she wondered if I was hurtling down a mountainside with failed brakes or in some other dangerous situation. After all, it was the middle of the day in the Philippines and she knew I was doing something important in the Lord's service.

Actually, at that moment I was sitting at my desk, while serving as director of a Bible college on the island of Mindanao. I had no sense of immediate crisis other than the fact that I was hurriedly preparing to teach my next class. Time was a precious commodity, and I did not find all the time I needed for my many responsibilities, so preparing my classes was always a challenge.

Fellow missionaries and Filipino church leaders repeatedly warned me that at the pace I was going in the tropics, I was approaching the breaking point. When I asked them what responsibilities I should give up, their faces went blank and no one offered any suggestions. I would gladly have shared some tasks with others, but the people around me were busy, too, or not trained to do some of the things on my agenda. I didn't want to let any of my ministries go undone.

I administered the Bible college affairs and staff, including training new teachers to prepare and present Bible school subjects. I taught a full load of classes, was preparing some courses for pastors, and was involved in many other mission responsibilities. Frequently, I traveled to speak in the churches in interior towns and villages.

Other missionaries were on medical leave, so we were short staffed. My tasks had multiplied, but I thought I could carry any load placed upon me. I tackled every job with a sense of purpose, because I knew I was serving the Lord. But was I realistic? Time would tell.

I did not realize I had used all my reserves. I burned the midnight oil night after night, and arose at 5:00 each morning. My colleagues were right. I was in danger. I was exhausted and stretched to the limit physically, emotionally, mentally, and spiritually. Yet, I was toughing it out, unwilling to admit the erosion of my energy and health.

When Grandma Wakeman rolled out of bed and knelt to intercede for me, she implored the Lord to meet my needs. Neither she nor I knew how close I was to the breaking point.

Sitting at my desk in the heat and humidity of the tropics, I wiped sweat from my face, neck, and arms. Though my concentration was intense, I realized someone had entered my office. Often, my secretary came in quietly, brought mail and papers, and retrieved what was in my outbox without saying a word while I was working. I assumed it was her. I was too involved to look up.

As I came to a stopping point in my work, I looked up to see who had entered my office. To my surprise, I saw no one. Yet I knew someone had come in.

Startled, I froze in a fear of the unknown. Then the mystery was solved. Slowly, sweetly, wonderfully I was overwhelmed by the presence of our living Lord, who had come to minister to me. He came in a way I had never experienced before.

My tense body relaxed. My tight emotions dissolved into tears of relief and joy. My cluttered mind became crystal clear as the Holy One invaded my spirit; He cleansed and filled and energized me through and through.

Wave after wave of divine love and power coursed through my being. I was renewed from my toes to the top of my head. My entire self—inside and out—was restored and invigorated in answer to Grandma Wakeman's intercession. God touched me in every aspect of my being. I was refreshed by His grace, empowered by His Spirit.

When those moments had passed, I glanced at my watch. It was time for my theology class. Never had I been better prepared for a class than I was at that moment. I picked up my class notes and went to a classroom filled with eager learners. I was surrounded by the presence of the One I taught about.

My words flowed with ease. I could see in the students' faces that they also sensed the Lord's presence.

For days I practically walked on tiptoes with renewed energy and resources. People noticed my new exuberance in my work. Those moments that renewed me had been so intimate, so precious that, like Mary, I treasured all these things and pondered them in my heart.

A year later, when our family returned on home assignment, I went to Grandma Wakeman's church to report on our mission work. After the service, I hugged her and asked the all-important question. "Grandma, have you ever awakened in the night to pray for me?"

"Oh yes," she replied warmly. "About a year ago I awoke with a feeling of urgency to pray for you. I sensed through the Holy Spirit that you were in some sort of crisis. I knelt by my bed and prayed earnestly, even with tears, until a sense of peace filled me. Then I got back into bed and went back to sleep."

We wept together as I told Grandma how God had used her to save me for continued ministry when I was at the end of my resources. I told her how the Lord answered her prayers and made a new person of me through His divine love and power. She glowed with joy to learn what had occurred as the result of her nighttime encounter with God.

Grandma Wakeman is an example of someone who let God have total control of her life. Her intimate walk with the Lord gave her a special sensitivity to the Holy Spirit's prompting. I'm grateful for that godly woman who now rejoices in the Holy One's presence. He used her life and prayers to save my ministry.

I've learned many lessons, but none more important than this: to live in communion with God so He can speak to me at any moment and prompt me to do His bidding.

the HEART-CHANGING PRAYER

Midge DeSart

When I met my husband in Bible College I thought we had a lot in common. He was from a family of seven children, and six kids were in my family. We assumed this meant we had similar upbringings.

Besides that, both of us had a strong faith, and had sung and played music in church services most of our lives. Ours was truly a match made in heaven. We were love struck. We couldn't see the storm clouds until about ten minutes after the ceremony. That was how long it took to realize that even though we came from large families our parents were poles apart in the way their families functioned.

My mom was a do-everything person. She did the cooking, the laundry, the cleaning, and the sewing, and taught an after-school Bible class for children. She was also head of the ladies missionary group at church and the church pianist.

Keith's mother was entirely different. She ran her home from a chair in the living room—like a queen bee directing the worker bees. The children did all laundry, ironing, and cleaning.

And if the children didn't finish their work, they couldn't go out and play. She was also president of the ladies mission group at her church.

Keith and I were headed for a major collision. "How can you not know how to cook?" He asked. "I thought you would know everything about housekeeping, and you don't know anything."

He was right. I couldn't even boil water–the pan went dry before I checked it. I had no experience in running a home. I'd never had to cook; my mom always did that. Who knew that playing the piano didn't prepare you for the real world?

When my talents fell short in the area of homemaking, Keith would remind me that his mother had taught him how to do the laundry, ironing, cleaning, and cooking–and he knew how to do it all the right way.

Only by the grace of God did we weather this storm. I was frequently humiliated until someone gave us a book on personalities and we learned we were a perfect couple–we both had something important to bring to our partnership. We began to focus on the compatible areas.

Keith was away from home a lot with his job and I became a happy homemaker. Life was smooth until our children began to grow up and we hit another traumatic clash of ideas on raising them. He wanted them to be involved in the housework while I didn't really care because I liked doing everything and enjoyed it when they went out to play. We had become our parents.

We both loved our children and wanted them to grow up happy, healthy, and loving the Lord. I always believed in the power of prayer. And when we had children my prayer life increased. The older they got, it seemed the more I prayed.

As a child I had been involved in lots of activities, such as piano recitals, school musicals, and singing in contests. My parents always supported everything anyone in the family did, and they made a point to be at all of our events.

Keith's family is also musical. Each child played at least one instrument. Keith played many and had been in concerts and parades most of his high school years. However, his parents didn't attend anyone's performances.

The big conflict finally came when our 13-year-old daughter, Melody, had a piano recital. Until then I had attended everything she had ever been involved in, field trips at school, choir concerts, plays, and cheerleader tryouts. When her recital was scheduled I knew it was important to her.

"Why doesn't Dad ever come to see me perform?" she asked.

I tried to make excuses for him because I couldn't tell her he didn't feel it was important.

When I asked him to come the recital he said, "My parents never attended my concerts and it didn't hurt me."

"I think it did," I said. "My parents always came to everything I was involved in and that's important for you to do for Melody."

About this time I was reading in Proverbs 19:13 where it says, "A quarrelsome wife is as annoying as constant dripping." Not wanting to be considered a Chinese water torturer, I didn't want to nag or manipulate him into attending. If it was important for my daughter to have her father at the recital, God knew it. I prayed to Melody's maker, who knew her needs, and asked Him to change my husband's heart.

I'm still astounded as I remember a conversation a day before the recital. Keith said, "Do you have any plans tomorrow?"

I said, "Yes, I'm going to Melody's recital."

"I think I'll go, too," he said.

Just like that. *What? Did I hear right? Why am I surprised that God answered my prayer?*

Keith did go and Melody, who is now a pastor's wife with four children of her own, has never forgotten. From that time on she was involved in plays, musicals, and many more recitals, and her father always attended with me. He was proud to let anyone in the room know that was his daughter.

God changed his heart. I'm just sorry I went to God as a last resort instead of a first responder.

MORE *than* WE ASKED FOR

Kevin Lucia

"We'll be late. We'll miss our appointment; we won't be able to reschedule." My wife fussed as she drove and I tried to get directions on the phone.

"Listen, the last person I talked to told me to go the opposite direction, so now . . . Honey, I'm talking to the receptionist and really can't . . . Yes, I'm still here. No, the other lady told me to go past the Arnot Mall and take a right, then follow the road all the way to the end and turn . . . . "

"I'm not kidding; I'm losing it over here!" my wife exclaimed,

"Daddy, are we at the doctor's yet?"

"Seriously. I can't take this right now, I really can't."

"Madison, we're almost there. Remember how we talked about being good so you can get some fries later? What's that? We should've turned left? Why did she tell us right? No, no, we're coming from Binghamton, not Corning."

"Kevin! Where. Are. We. Going?"

It was a good question. One God seemed to be withholding an answer to.

It's not easy to reassure your wife and put your four-year-old daughter at ease while getting contradictory directions from receptionists who obviously had no idea what "white-knuckled mother driving way over the speed limit" meant.

This appointment at the Elmira satellite site of Rochester's Strong Memorial Hospital had been an answer to prayer. Now it seemed that answer was being trampled on by bored-sounding receptionists. After waiting months for an appointment, we were late and lost. If we missed it, we'd have to wait even longer, after going through the emotional rigors of getting ourselves—and Madison—prepared for our trip.

Madison had been contently watching cartoons on her portable DVD, but we had no idea how long that would last. Before that we'd struggled with her for a while. At that point, even if we did arrive, we'd be late, Madison would be nigh uncontrollable, and the whole trip would be for nothing.

At that moment, I uttered a silent prayer I'm sure many before me have prayed: *God, what are You doing?*

We'd expressed that question frequently in the previous year as we'd struggled to accept a fact no parent wants to face: our child was different. At home, she was a remarkably literate, polite, bright, and charming four-year-old. In public, she was high-strung and emotionally erratic. Her attention span was fragmented, her behavior often compulsive and repetitive. Overly sensitive to loud noises and external stimuli, our daughter was not—perish the thought—normal.

Through various therapies and evaluations, we'd learned much. However, we'd also come to a breaking point. Since our son had been born, our lives had turned into barely-managed chaos. Our children consumed our lives. We required a rigid schedule to keep order, which precluded any social life with friends or even each other.

Grocery shopping was akin to traveling through Dante's Inferno, as were family gatherings. My wife and I were both exhausted; she often felt embarrassed at our inability to control Madison, while I moved through the day of teaching school like a zombie. Worse, as we studied parents with similar aged children, we realized that comparatively speaking, our experience wasn't the norm.

Something was wrong. Badly.

Our goal at that appointment was clear. We needed to know one thing. Though her therapy had shown promise, a nagging suspicion lingered. We needed the truth, no matter what it was, though that truth revolved around one word that threatened to turn our world upside down: *autism.*

Prayer is an odd thing. Sometimes we get what we ask for. Often, prayer is answered in unimagined ways. Occasionally, though, prayers are answered in ways that open doors to new burdens, which then returns us to the original question: *God, what are You doing? Where are we going?*

Luckily, the second receptionist gave better directions. We made it to our appointment in time. Madison was in a good mood, my wife was clutching the steering wheel less tightly, and collectively we relaxed. However, that dark thing called "autism" still loomed. What would happen today? What would this diagnosis mean for us and most importantly, our daughter?

We were ushered into our appointment. The doctor was smart, insightful, and straightforward. She played casual games with Madison while talking to us. We filled out various surveys and answered many questions about Madison's likes, dislikes, quirks, traits, and fears.

"Now, do you see this?" the doctor whispered as Madison transitioned from playing with some Slinkies to lining up farm animals and talking with each one of them. "This is not only independent thought, but very organized, interactive play."

She turned to us with a smile. "There is some repetitive behavior here, and occasionally her speech sounds recorded, rote. But this isn't autism. She certainly has behavioral needs that will require intervention for several years, and will also require a strong united front by both of you. But your daughter is not autistic."

Anyone who hasn't been in that situation has no idea what those words meant to us. Our prayers were answered, but as the doctor further explained autism's symptoms, I looked at my wife, and knew we thought the same thing. Our prayers about Madison had been answered dramatically, but we'd also gotten an answer to a question we hadn't asked, or perhaps had shied away from asking, afraid of the answer.

Our two-year-old son, Zackary. Though he was also bright, energetic, interactive, and loving, he wasn't speaking yet. He'd just started speech therapy, which our friends assured us would be quickly successful, and we'd hoped that his behavior was merely an imitation of big sister Madison's.

Zack smiled. He played. He sought us out for his needs, even though he wasn't speaking yet. He wasn't autistic. Was he?

In our answer to prayer, we'd been given another, perhaps even greater challenge and burden.

If Madison had been autistic she would've had the "best" kind, Asperger's Syndrome. She was highly intelligent, verbal, and expressive. She could clearly communicate her needs. Her behavioral quirks—though overwhelming at times—were largely emotional and social. We could teach her many things.

Zack was non-verbal. He displayed tendencies and lapses that, until that point, we'd attributed to his speech deficiencies. Our answer to prayer had given us new cause for worry: While Madison was not autistic, we realized Zackary perfectly fit the profile for autism.

On top of this, Madison still had needs. She was harder to control than most children in public, easily excitable and emotional. She required a "brushing protocol," which entailed brushing her entire body with a small, rectangular brush every two hours to keep her relaxed, no matter where we were. Missing a "brushing" meant the difference between night and day in her behavior. She needed a "weighted blanket" to help her sleep at night and during naps so we could sleep.

And now, Zack had even greater needs that would require even more intervention.

In the middle of answered prayer, a sobering realization hit us: we were parents of two special needs children. Once again the prayer came to mind: *God, what are You doing?*

We drove home in a mixture of relief and somber thought, both of us happy about Madison's diagnosis, but also searching ourselves—and God—for a way to deal with what came next: evaluating Zack for autism.

"You know," I said as we left for the hour-long trip home. "If Zack is autistic, we'll deal. Actually, we're perfect for this."

I remember the look my wife gave me. It wasn't skeptical, but she certainly wasn't sure what I meant. "How?"

"Well, I've been thinking. You're a nurse. I'm a teacher. Before teaching, what type of kids did I mainly work with?"

She nodded slowly. "Autistic kids."

"Right. Here's something else, too—how many of those folks you've been e-mailing and talking with on Facebook about Madison have autistic children?"

She glanced at me and I could almost see the wheels and gears turning in her head. "All of them," she answered quietly.

"I know this won't be easy, and Zack will be much harder to deal with than Madison . . . but our prayers for him have already been answered. Everything we need is in place. God has put us right where we need to be."

Our ride home was quiet. Madison enjoyed her DVDs, I got some reading done, and my wife and I did some pretty serious thinking about the future, which was enriched with the realization that adopting an attitude of continuous prayer had not only put us in the best frame of mind to accept challenges like these, but it had provided answers to problems that we had never imagined in the first place.

Several months later, our son was diagnosed as "severely autistic." Even prepared as we were, the diagnosis carried with it all the expected baggage. Our lives had been mapped out for the next several years, and the terrain looked rocky, and in some cases, near treacherous. And yet, God's unexpected answer had far-reaching, equally unexpected results.

The first was the discovery that Zack's social worker was not only a young woman of faith, but had attended a Christian high school I'd taught at. Abby's network of friends with autistic and special needs children grew to the point that my old classmates, who didn't even know her, e-mailed her, offering support.

We discovered that Zack's new caseworker with the local chapter of the Handicapped Children's Association was also a person of faith. So was Zack's speech therapist, whom he adored and who worked God's power directly into our lives and Zack's.

Perhaps the ultimate answer to our question of *God, what are You doing?* came when I recently passed my wife busily typing away on the computer, looking content and perhaps even joyful. I assumed she was chatting with her mother or sister, or shopping, but when I asked what she was doing, I received the best answer to our prayers that I ever could have.

"I'm e-mailing a mother who just learned her son is autistic. She doesn't know how to deal with it, so I'm showing her how." She looked at me. Something bright glimmered in her eyes. "It's something I know all about."

Perhaps that's the true power of answered prayer. Not what we get from it, but what it empowers us to give to others.

a KISS of FAITH

Genell Dawson

Late one Sunday afternoon the phone rang. My husband, Clyde, had promised to be home ages ago.

What now? I thought.

"Maybe Dad stopped to buy you a birthday present," Amber, my daughter, suggested, picking up the receiver. I rolled my eyes. My birthday was still five days away, and Amber knew just as well as I did that Clyde always put off buying gifts until the last minute. I checked my watch. Already 4:30. Typical workaholic Clyde. If he wasn't logging overtime as a facilitics cnginccr at thc local Toyota plant like today, he was working through our church, even spending his last few vacations on mission trips in Mexico and Russia.

Amber turned to me, a strange look on her face, and held out the phone. "It's Mission Hospital," she said. "They want to talk to you—about Dad."

Clyde had been in a car accident. I was praying for him before I even hung up the phone. Amber and I jumped into the car. I rattled off numbers as I drove. Rev. Dudley Bristow from our old church; my boss and good friend, Janet; people from our current congregation. Amber called them on the cell.

Lately it seemed Clyde and I spent what little time we did have together arguing about the time we spent apart. We always kissed and made up in the end, though. After almost twenty years, that simple act was still a powerful reminder of the love that had drawn us together. *Please, God,* I prayed, pulling up to the hospital, *give us more time.*

The chaplain came to talk to us. "Your husband has been critically injured and is in surgery," she said. "You need to get his family here as soon as you can."

Amber and I made more frantic calls. Our older daughter, Michelle, at college in Arizona. Clyde's twin brother, Curt, and their older brother, Jerry. Our family physician and friend, Dr. Pino. One thought kept going through my mind: *Was Clyde still alive?* In the background the same prayer repeated steadily like a heartbeat: *Please, God, give us more time.*

By 1:00 AM more than one hundred family and friends were gathered in the waiting area. Finally a surgeon with blood on his scrubs, his deeply lined eyes just visible over his mask, emerged from the operating suite and took me aside. "Mrs. Dawson, your husband has suffered grave injuries. He's been lacerated from his ribs to his pelvic bone back to his spine. His stomach, liver, and kidneys are badly damaged. We've done everything we can, but he's in a coma. I'm very sorry, but I don't think he will make it through the night."

All that got through to me at that moment was that Clyde was still alive. And that meant he could be healed. "I have my faith," I said.

The doctor sighed. “You’re going to need more than that, I’m afraid,” he said.

I’d relied on my faith my entire life, taking strength in knowing that God could help me through anything. Now my husband was dying and his doctor was telling me not even God could save his life. What if it really was too late? What if there was nothing more even God could do? The prayer circling my mind continued, longer now. *Please, God, give us more time. Give me whatever I need to help Clyde.*

They let me see Clyde. I could hardly tell where tubes and machines ended and he began. Since he had a tube down his throat I couldn’t kiss him, and I had to wear protective gloves just to touch him.

When I reached to stroke his brow, the nurse stopped me. “Be careful. His bones are fractured,” she said.

I drew back and choked out, “I’m sorry,” and then I fled to the waiting room.

I couldn’t sleep, even with a sedative. Thank goodness my sister-in-law had brought my Bible and prayer journal.

The nurses allowed me five minutes of visiting time each hour and at first that was all I could bear. During the day Amber or Michelle or a friend from church would go into the ICU with me. At night it was just Clyde and me. The more I sat with my husband the harder it was to leave when the nurses asked.

On the third night, I pulled off the gloves, hoping Clyde would respond to my touch. I stroked his cheek, his forehead, the scraggly hair growing out of his chin. “Keep holding on, Baby,” I whispered. “Only twenty more days until our twentieth anniversary.” I even wrote that in my journal.

The fifth day I remarked to a nurse as I sat with Clyde, "The doctor didn't think he'd make it through the first night. Maybe he'll wake up soon."

The nurse touched my shoulder. "Mrs. Dawson, I think it's important you understand your husband is still in very critical condition," she said. "He's on dialysis, his spleen has been removed, and his other organs are shutting down one by one. I'm sorry, but he's far from waking up."

Back in the waiting room friends and family surprised me with a cake. My birthday. How could I celebrate my birth when my husband was dying? I excused myself to talk to Dr. Pino. "Please, you've got to be honest with me," I begged him.

He shook his head. "Genell, prepare for the worst."

I felt my knees buckle. Only through the most intense prayer had I been able to keep it together these past five days. But things were getting worse, not better. Clyde was still holding on. How would I? *God, I don't know how to pray any harder. Give me more faith.*

The nurses stopped asking me to leave after five minutes. I bathed and shaved Clyde as best I could around the tubes and bandages. "You're wasting away. Wouldn't you like to wake up and have a chile relleno right now?" I asked. One day I pressed his hand to my lips. "You already missed my birthday. You don't want to miss our anniversary, too, do you?"

I felt so connected to him that it seemed like his body was an extension of my own, that it was my breath flowing into him.

It was the same way with my prayers. I prayed so deeply that prayer became less of an act than a state of being. And I was surrounded by hundreds of others who were praying fervently for my husband's recovery—relatives, friends, our church family, even people in Mexico and Russia whom Clyde had met on his mission trips. We prayed for Clyde's organs one by one. "Help Clyde's kidneys work again, Lord. Heal the damage to his liver." We prayed for his foot and the doctors saved it even though it was broken in dozens of places and had become gangrenous.

Another five days passed, but now I knew better than to think that meant Clyde was out of the woods. Instead I took joy in the little things. Like being able to kiss him again. A tracheotomy allowed the tube to come out of his throat at last. His facial muscles were still tensed up in a grimace so I massaged around his mouth, hoping to ease it into a smile.

"I love you, Clyde. I'm sorry about all the times we ever argued," I said. "Please wake up, Baby."

I rested my head on the pillow beside his. And I felt not Clyde but God answer me. *Be still and trust me.*

On day 21 I went home to shower, but then it was right back to the ICU, to Clyde. I nodded to the nurse and turned to look at my husband. I'd just given him a bath and shave, and he looked rested. I bent to kiss him hello like always. Just before I pulled away, I thought I felt his lips move.

I drew back and stared at him. His eyes were still closed. Again I kissed him. He puckered up and kissed me back! Clyde had kissed me back! And that kiss was a promise, just like the kiss that sealed our wedding vows twenty years earlier. Except this time the promise was not so much from Clyde as from God—a promise that He was returning my husband to me, that He was giving us more time after all.

"Nurse, my husband kissed me!"

"It's likely just a reflex," she said.

"No, watch," I insisted. I kissed Clyde and again he puckered his lips and kissed me back.

The nurse's eyes widened. "I have to get the doctor."

I kissed Clyde twice more before the doctor came. Then I kissed him again. He kissed me back. The doctor squeezed Clyde's hand. He squeezed back. Later that same day Clyde started to wake up. Two days later, on October 31, we marked our twentieth anniversary. "We'll spend much more of the next twenty years together, won't we, Baby?" I asked. Clyde still couldn't talk, but for me his kiss was answer enough.

I'd sat by my husband's bedside those long days not knowing if he would wake up again. The doctor had been right. My faith had not been enough. But all I had to do was reach out and ask, and I received more than I ever could have imagined. God gives us faith as generously as he gives his love. And both know no bounds.

a DATE *with* GOD

Chrissy Ogden Marsh

Annie, my eight-year-old, pushed the makeshift cross of twigs and twine into the fresh dirt covering the tiny grave next to our old shed. We'd done the right thing, rescuing Helen. That's what Annie had named the injured loon we found on the beach the night before. Not that there was any other choice but to try to save the dying bird, not with a passionate kid like my Annie.

But I worried. Hadn't she and her five-year-old sister, Lily, already faced too great a loss? Their dad and I had endured a difficult divorce. Afterward, I had decided to move with the girls from New Mexico to North Carolina. The three of us needed a new beginning.

"I forgot something!" Annie said as our prayer ended. She ran to the house and came back waving her favorite pink glitter pen in one hand and a letter she'd written in the other.

Annie set the letter beside the grave. I knelt to take a closer look. "Dear God, I hope you are doing good," it read. "What is it like in heaven? Can you write back and tell me? And, God, I love you. Thank you, God, for letting me be in the world. Thank you, God, for making me part of my family. And thank you, God, for letting me be me. Love, Annie."

My girls had gone to church all their lives. I tried to instill a strong faith in them, a faith they could depend on throughout their lives.

Yet now I found myself wondering about the strength of my own faith. The pain of my divorce was very much with me. I was still angry. The stress of moving, unpacking, and getting the girls settled in a new school had left me feeling like I'd put God on hold. Meanwhile my daughter was writing him letters. Not make-believe letters either. Annie expected an answer.

Every time we left the house over the next few days, Annie and Lily dashed to Helen's grave to say a prayer. "It goes directly to heaven and into a big prayer book," Annie explained to her sister one day. "And then God calls out Helen's name and she comes over and reads her new prayer." Lily nodded her curly head in earnest agreement.

The next morning we were in a rush to get to school. "C'mon, girls," I said. "We gotta run." I helped them into their coats and shut the porch door behind us.

"But we need to say a prayer," Lily protested. "For Helen."

"Short and sweet," I said.

The girls raced through a prayer. I urged them to the car.

"Wait!" Annie said, snatching something off the damp ground. "What's this?"

It was a letter, next to the one she'd written.

"Dear Annie, I love you," she read aloud. "Yes, heaven is a wonderful place. It is made of gold and there are angels everywhere. Love, your best friend, God."

Annie's reading slowed with each word. Her eyes widened with awe, her mouth opened in amazement.

Whoever did this means well, I thought, *but I don't have a good feeling about it.*

By the time Annie burst through the door that afternoon, she couldn't wait to tell me her plan. Dropping her Barbie backpack to the floor, she said, "Know what? I'm going to write God another letter and I'm going to ask Him to meet me in the backyard so we can play!"

Just what I'd been afraid of. I didn't want to discourage Annie, but I couldn't stand by and watch my daughter set herself up for disappointment. She had so much trust. Divorce had taught me that too much trust can be a dangerous thing.

Before I knew it she was at the kitchen table, jacket still on, scribbling intently. She ended with, "Please try and meet me in the shed in a half hour. Love, Annie."

I watched through the window as she raced out and left the letter by Helen's grave, with a blank piece of paper and her pink glitter pen, presumably so God could reply.

She ran back inside and into her room, only to return wearing the special white dress she put on for big occasions, with the bow in back.

"Tie my bow for me, Mom!" she said. "Please! I've got to get ready for God!"

She brushed her hair until it shone, put on her favorite sparkly headband and zoomed back out. Next time I glanced out the window, Annie was solemnly sitting on the back porch steps. I got up to join her and noticed two kitchen chairs were missing.

"You okay?" I asked.

"He hasn't shown up yet, Mom." She adjusted her headband and slumped her little shoulders.

"Sweetie, nobody ever gets to really see God except when they go to heaven, and you're too young to go."

Annie didn't buy it. She brightened when she spotted an older man strolling up the street. Perhaps he was God? I had to tell her he was just a neighbor, and then asked, "You don't know where those kitchen chairs are, do you?"

Annie led me to the shed. I creaked open the door. There were my two kitchen chairs. Annie had emptied out everything else—the bicycles, the scooters, and the old stroller—and placed the chairs face-to-face, waiting for God. I held her hand as we walked slowly back to the porch. Later I brought her dinner out.

Annie came inside when the sun had set, changed into her Tweety Bird pajamas, and brushed her teeth.

"I've been thinking, Mom," she confided to me as she got into bed. "I can still write and pray to God anytime, right?"

"Anytime," I assured, tucking her in with a hug. "God is always there so you can always talk to Him."

I watched Annie fall asleep, content and peaceful, then checked in on Lily. She was sleeping soundly too. I threw on a sweater and trudged across the yard to drag the chairs back in from the shed.

I flipped on the light and went inside. But instead of grabbing the chairs, I sat. How long had it been since I'd reached out to God with the same pure and passionate faith as my daughter?

"Maybe you and I need to talk," I said to the chair opposite me. I sat there, letting my anger, disappointment, and fear pour out, handing it all over to God.

Yes, You are always with me, I prayed. *Through the difficulty of divorce, through the challenge of starting over. Always.*

A long time might pass before my heart healed. I understood that. But I knew what I needed to do.

"God," I asked, "help me to trust again." Rain fell softly and rhythmically against the shed roof. It sounded like peace.

We never found out who wrote the note to Annie, and we like it that way. It was probably a neighbor or maybe a classmate who walked by Helen's grave on the way to school. But I do know one thing since I overheard Annie on the phone with her grandmother. "Grandma, don't tell anyone I said this," she had lowered her voice to a whisper, "but God doesn't really have very good handwriting."

I'll bet Grandma smiled. I did. And I'm pretty sure I felt God smiling on us, too.

KNOWING WHERE *to turn*

Thomas J. Haggai

Challenges have always made my adrenaline surge, but one blustery January day a long time ago I wondered if I could measure up to the new one that faced me.

Inside the Chicago O'Hare Marriott Hotel I was greeted by Dick Harrison and Ted Wetterau, chairman and vice chairman of IGA, Inc. (formerly Independent Grocers Alliance). Since 1926, IGA had licensed family-owned supermarkets throughout the U.S. and Canada. But now the corporation faced serious trouble. Some predicted it might fail. Dick and Ted were preparing to hold an emergency meeting of the board of directors.

And they had asked that I meet with the company executives.

As I walked to the meeting room I wondered what I had to say to these men. They were all senior executive officers of the firms that owned IGA. They needed a businessman, a financier, and a strategist, certainly not a man like me. Yet all my life I had tried to be faithful to a commitment I had made when I was just a boy: I had promised God that as He opened doors I would do my best by His strength to respond to the opportunities.

I slipped back in time to being a 12-year-old lad in Boston's infamous Scollay Square. I could see myself standing on the back of a truck with a choir and a pulpit, preaching to the World War II servicemen who had come to the red-light district. They were looking for one kind of gratification, but we hoped to exhort them to find something better.

I was a PK, a preacher's kid, and wanted the soldiers and sailors to know they weren't to look back and live in guilt of the past, but rather to accept the love of God, which is all-forgiving and all-strengthening. I emphasized that they could feel his love personally through prayer as I had experienced it.

Earlier that year I had not been able to eat for several days because of a serious intestinal blockage that would require surgery. During the final exam, before the doctor scheduled the operation, I blurted out, "I sure would like to have a glass of milk and a cookie."

The physician, knowing I had not been able to eat for several days, turned to the nurse and said, "This youngster certainly has retained his sense of humor, hasn't he?" He then probed my abdomen, winked at the nurse, and said, "Well, let's put him to a test. Bring him a cookie and milk." She did. I hungrily ate it and digested it.

The doctor X-rayed me again, developed the film, and said, "No way to explain it–it's a miracle. The blockage has cleared."

While my family was having dinner that evening, the doorbell rang and the man at the door said, "I just had to come by, pastor. I was in your audience at noon when you spoke at our meeting today and asked us to remember your son in prayer. I wanted to find out what the latest word is."

He rejoiced with the good news, and as he and Dad talked, they realized that at the same time the five hundred laymen were praying for me in Boston, I was asking the doctor for a cookie and milk.

Coincidence? Well, as the late evangelist Rodney "Gypsy" Smith of England said, "You may call it coincidence, and if I'm dreaming, just let me dream on."

Seven years later, while attending Furman University in Greenville, South Carolina, I listened to a missionary pleading for starving children in his area. All I had was a five-dollar bill to tide me over until my parents sent the little bit they could give me each week. Yet as I pictured the faces of those starving children I realized how blessed I was. So my last five dollars found its way into the offering plate.

For some reason my weekly letter from Mom didn't arrive. Saturday became 24 hours of forced fasting. On Sunday I was at the church where I served as student assistant and recreation planner for the young people.

At the close of the morning worship service the pastor announced, "Our fine young assistant pastor has not seen his parents for some while, and I think we should send him to spend time with Mom and Dad. If you want to share in this, I've asked an usher to be at the main door of the sanctuary."

The money given was far more than I would need for meals, and certainly plenty for gas to drive home. Moreover, a couple in the congregation in the car business decided I should have a new car with a full tank of gas to make the trek.

Those were my thoughts as I took a deep breath and walked into the IGA meeting room full of solemn-faced executives.

Almost immediately the chairman called for my comments. I said, "Gentlemen, you are not broke; you are just out of money. There is a tremendous difference. When I'm in a position such as yours, and don't know what to do, I turn to God, and I feel there are times when just bowing my head isn't as satisfactory as actually getting on my knees in prayer. This may be the most appropriate action we could take together today."

For a moment a shocked silence permeated the boardroom. But then, one by one, the men eased to their knees on the carpet. I too knelt, remembering an old saying: "On one knee, God gets half a person: on two He gets him all."

"Oh, Lord," I prayed, "give these men a vision beyond the immediate crisis. Help them understand that You are even more concerned than they are about themselves and their obligations. And, Lord, if any of them does not have enough faith to meet this challenge, give him some of mine, for despite all my weaknesses, I have no doubt that God plus one makes a majority."

When the prayer was finished I reminded them that IGA wasn't broke, it was just temporarily out of money. I reassured them that as they combined their wisdom and experience they would know what steps to take, even if it meant sacrifices.

The vice chairman took it from there, and before long the sun began to break through the clouds once again upon the company that J. Frank Grimes had founded several decades earlier.

After that meeting I had no idea I would be asked to join the board. But before long, I was elected vice chairman and, two years later, chairman. Then I became CEO.

Now I serve as IGA Global president, chairman and CEO, and non-executive chairman of IGA, INC.

Today there are more than four thousand IGA stores worldwide.

As part of my job I travel the world, and invariably someone will ask, "Why did you leave the ministry?"

My reply has always been the same, "This is my ministry. It is the same I pledged to God as a lad, that if he would open the door, I would walk in." Every morning I wake up excited, believing I can do something that day to help our stores become more effective in serving people with compassion and caring.

Yes, it is a triumphant God who is always present with us, even at the boardroom table.

CHASING *a* PRODIGAL FATHER

Julie Saffrin

"Julie, I can't find Dad!" my mother sobbed over the phone.

Dad had been in the hospital with a transient ischemic attack the week before Christmas. After he was released the minor stroke had left him tired but feeling well enough to enjoy celebrating Christmas.

Now two days later, Dad had had a rough night. He'd had Alzheimer's for ten years, and the symptoms of the disease repeatedly jolted him awake. At 3:00 AM my mom, his exhausted caregiver, had moved to sleep in the bedroom across the hall. She woke up at 6:00 AM and discovered he was not in bed. She looked everywhere but found no sign of her husband of forty years.

Because of the Alzheimer's, Mom always dead-bolted the exit doors to keep Dad housebound. On this morning, the key had been in the back door, but it had been unlocked. She had next run to the kitchen to where she had hidden his car keys.

Dad's wallet was on the counter. His keys were gone. She clicked the garage door opener to their detached garage. As the door wheels climbed the track, she burst into tears. That's when she phoned me.

"The whole house is lit like a Christmas tree," she explained. "The Nissan isn't in the garage. Your dad is gone!"

"I'm on my way, Mom," I said and threw on jeans, a shirt, and a coat. I asked my husband to wake up our three boys and meet me at my parents' house, 25 miles away.

Many Alzheimer's victims are wanderers but Dad had always been content at home. Mom took him for rides and to their Lutheran church on Sundays. Though he couldn't remember anyone's name, he was friendly to everyone. Of Cornish descent, Dad was a quiet, humble man with a dry sense of humor. He told people the one joke his memory had left him at least 15 times a day.

I pulled up to my childhood home. A squad car and other cars were in the driveway. My brother Mark, his wife, and four children were in the family room with Mom. Jenny, my sister-in-law, had her arm around Mom, who sat in Dad's recliner.

"His robe is in the closet," Mom said to the officer. "I think he's only wearing his pajamas and slippers." Silently I thanked God for the unseasonably warm forty-degree temperature.

The officer wrote the information on the Missing Persons Report and asked for a physical description.

"He has blue eyes and is six feet, 180 pounds and seventy years old." Mom rubbed her folded arms and choked back tears. "He hasn't driven for a year, with his memory being so bad. He's been so weak. If I had thought, even for a second, that something like this could happen . . . . " She wiped her eyes and blew her nose. "He was so proud of his car. He loved to drive. He's had so many things stripped from him. I didn't want to take away his dignity by taking away his keys."

No one wanted to say what we had just discussed at Christmas. On a regular basis Dad now talked about his mother as though he had spoken with her the day before. He had forgotten he lived in Bloomington, Minnesota, and thought he still lived in a home, long sold, just outside of Eau Claire, Wisconsin.

"Don," Mom would lovingly say to him, "Your mother died twenty years ago. Don't you remember?"

Dad would squint hard and nod reluctantly.

"Any idea where he might have gone?" the officer, dressed in the navy uniform asked.

Mom looked at us and said, "I think Don might try to go back to what used to be his mother's house in Wisconsin."

With one look, Mark and I telegraphed our thoughts to each other. *Would Dad really attempt to drive one hundred miles when he had no idea how to get to the gas station five blocks away?*

The officer wrote a list of places we thought Dad might go and left, promising to contact us should he hear anything.

"Mom, I think you and I should head for Eau Claire," Mark said. My other brother Steve, and his family, phoned from their Wisconsin cabin. They would head toward Eau Claire from the opposite direction, and hopefully, between the two vehicles, someone would spot Dad on the interstate.

By 7:15 AM everyone except me departed in search of a lost man in a city of two million. My sister-in-law left with her children. My husband called to say he and the boys were looking too. I was to hold down the fort and promised to call everyone if the police found Dad.

Feeling helpless, I downed coffee, but with everyone gone, every creak in the house put me on edge. I felt prompted to call my friend Sue and ask, "Can you come sit with me?" She arrived twenty minutes later and her presence calmed my shattered nerves.

An hour went by. The phone rang. Mark was calling from a gas station sixty miles away. "Mom heard an All Points Bulletin for Dad on the police radio while I was paying for gasoline."

We were comforted that the authorities were taking Dad's being lost seriously. I hung up and turned to Sue.

"This is the most attention my father has received in his life and he doesn't even know these are his 15 minutes of fame."

She laughed. "God has your dad in His hands."

Lately Dad had been prone to falling in and out of sleep throughout the day. I tried not to think about him snoozing behind the wheel, grateful it was a Saturday morning with fewer cars on the roads.

I wanted to keep the house line clear and used my cell phone to call my friend Mary around nine o'clock.

"I'll pray someone spots Don," she said. I called my husband's brother Bob. "I'm praying that your dad gets hungry and stops to eat somewhere."

I was so glad for their prayers.

Those on the road checked in regularly to see if I had heard anything. My brother, Steve, now in a northern suburb of the Twin Cities, called to say the Nissan wasn't at the office Dad had retired from 11 years earlier. Jenny called from the nearby Mall of America parking lot. Dad had once loved to shop for tools, but a search for him at Sears turned up nothing.

The phone call I longed for wasn't coming.

God, I prayed, *only You know where Dad is. Help us find him. Please guide him to safety.*

Another hour dragged by. Mark and Mom called from Eau Claire. With no sign of Dad at the old family homestead, they stopped at Dad's friend's home. No luck. I updated the rest of the family. The family pastor called to let me know the congregation had been notified and was praying.

Looking outside the living room window at the melting snow, I thought of Dad in his thin cotton pajamas. I hoped he remembered how to turn on the car's heater.

Suddenly, at 11 AM, the house phone rang.

"Is this Julie?" a male voice asked.

I found it odd that someone would ask for me at my parents' house. I hadn't lived there for nearly twenty years.

"Yes," I said, tentatively.

"Home of Donald Trewartha?"

"Yes," I gulped. "I'm his daughter."

"This is Officer Reynolds. We have your father here at Big Olaf's in downtown Minneapolis."

I had to smile that Dad would provide us comic relief by stopping at a Norwegian restaurant. Relieved that he was found, I explained what had transpired that morning. I asked the officer how he knew to dial this number because Dad hadn't taken his wallet with his name and emergency information in it.

"The restaurant owner asked your father who they should call. He said, 'Call my daughter, Julie' and gave us this number."

I was amazed that Dad had remembered my name and his phone number!

Thank you, God, I said in silence, *for having me stay at the house to take phone calls.*

"Is he okay?" I finally asked.

"Oh yes. A couple saw him in the parking lot rummaging through the trunk. Because he was only wearing a sweater they called the police, but not before they gave him breakfast." The officer chuckled. "We'll get his car to the station just as soon as he's finished eating. Why don't you come for him there?"

I took down the directions to the police station and hung up.

Sue and I hugged. I called Elsie and Keith, my parents' best friends, and they agreed to meet me at the station so that they could drive my car back to my parents' home, enabling me to drive the Nissan back. Sue stayed at the house to share the good news with family now scattered throughout the city.

Driving downtown, I thanked God for all He had done that morning. The situation was out of our control, yet God had worked on our behalf. He had prompted and answered Mary and Bob's specific prayers—that Dad would get hungry and be seen. And when Dad was seen, strangers provided a meal for him and law enforcement officers kept him safe.

Though Dad had been lost, our heavenly Father had used a variety of friends, family, and community members to bring Dad back to us.

I arrived at the station to find my father in a chair, wearing corduroy pants, cardigan, and moccasins. His blue-and-white striped pajamas peeked from under his sweater and pants legs. His gray curly hair was uncombed. His baby blue eyes had dark circles beneath them. He seemed unsure why he was sitting there. I swallowed hard. "Hi, Dad."

"Well, hi, Julie!" he said, breaking into a grin. "How did you know to find me here?"

I wanted to tell him but knew he couldn't absorb it. I hugged him, taking in my father's scent. Elsie and Keith arrived and I gave them my keys.

An officer handed me Dad's key chain. "Probably time he didn't have access to these anymore," he said. The corners of his mouth turned in an upside-down smile.

I wiped my cheeks and nodded.

I guided Dad's tired body into the passenger side of the Nissan then got in on the driver's side. How he found the energy to get dressed and drive for hours would forever remain unsolved. I was glad the mystery of my missing father was solved and that he was unharmed by the adventure.

Dad and I arrived home to hugs of happiness from family and friends. All of us celebrated the return of a Cornishman we had chased in two states, grateful to the Almighty for answered prayers and thankful that He brought our beloved prodigal back to the fold.

HELP ME LOVE MY HUSBAND

Kitty Chappell

I collapsed to my knees before God one stormy night, sobbing. I trembled as the terrible words tumbled out in their raw, naked honesty, "I don't love my husband anymore."

My heart felt as tumultuous as the weather outside. The wind howled, moaning its discontent, matching the mood of my soul. Lightning punctuated the unspoken sentences cringing in the dark crevices of my mind. My husband was sleeping upstairs in our bedroom, oblivious of my soul's turmoil.

Twenty-plus years earlier, Jerry and I had gazed into each other's love-filled eyes and agreed "until death do us part." But now, that love for him lay dead at my feet—trampled by who knows what.

How could this happen? By all appearances, ours was the perfect Christian marriage. Not my family, not our teenage children, not even my closest friend suspected otherwise.

I'm sure Jerry knew something was wrong, but not even he would guess the ugly truth. How could any Christian woman admit such a personal flaw to anyone—especially since I didn't have a specific reason? Jerry didn't abuse me and he'd never been unfaithful.

I can't recall what first prompted my dissatisfaction—our midlife crises, dealing with two teenagers, financial pressures, or just the wear-and-tear of married life. Maybe I had expected too much. How could any husband compete with the handsome lovers performing perfectly according to script in the romantic movies I loved to watch?

Could it have stemmed from my painful past with a violent and abusive father? Or was it just my own self-centeredness? Who knows? But nothing Jerry did pleased me.

It's not that I didn't have valid complaints. At times Jerry was insensitive, thoughtless, and downright cold. Worse, he rarely complimented me—something my low self-esteem craved. As I daily reviewed my husband's real and perceived shortcomings, they multiplied and grew stronger. So did my discontent.

Time and again, I complained to God. "Lord, I don't like feeling this way, but my husband has changed. He isn't the attentive, loving, and sensitive man he once was. I try to be a godly wife, but a good wife loves her husband—for better or worse. And quite frankly, I don't like his 'worse.' I miss the man I married. Would You touch Jerry's heart, soften it, and change him into the man he once was so I can love him again and be the model Christian wife everyone thinks I am?"

For two long years I prayed that prayer, but heaven remained silent and my husband remained unchanged.

I grew more miserable with each day, until I finally fell to my knees in despair that stormy night. "I can't take it anymore, Lord! I can't bear the thought of living in a loveless marriage for the rest of my life. But I certainly don't want a divorce. My marriage is a lifetime commitment, but right now it truly feels like a death sentence."

Emotionally spent, I hiccupped a sob and crawled on the couch where I lay in a curled position. The thunder rumbled off into the distance, and the lightning found interests elsewhere. For a long time I listened to the patter of the rain on the roof, and waited in silence.

Finally, in resignation I added, "Lord, if You will not change Jerry, will You please change me and help me love him as he is? I don't know what else to do," I admitted, sighing. "I believe You can do this because You helped me to forgive my abusive father—and I felt that was impossible. Please help me love my husband as I once did."

This became my daily prayer.

Gradually I realized that I was to play an active role in prayer. I'd always expected God to do it all without my involvement, especially when it came to people and circumstances. My role was to pray and God's role was to answer. Right? Change the people and change my circumstances so I could be happy. Didn't I deserve that? And when things didn't happen the way I wanted, I became discouraged, sometimes I got angry with God.

What happened next bears a truth every Christian knows deep inside—God often answers prayer in unexpected ways.

I had recently become interested in the power of "self-talk," which is the things we say to ourselves, day in and day out, all of our lives. I had acquired a dynamic tape series by a Christian motivational speaker friend that encouraged listeners to control their self-talk.

The tape series entered my life at the perfect time. One tape challenged the listeners to a mental exercise. We were to select someone who irritated us—a mate, boss, coworker, relative, friend, whomever—and think no critical thoughts about that person for thirty days.

At that time, it was my husband, of course, who irritated me the most. I asked God for strength and accepted that challenge.

"Because all nature abhors a vacuum," the motivational speaker said, "you must fill the empty space in your mind—space your negative thoughts once occupied—with positive thoughts. Make a list of every good quality you can think of about that person and read them throughout the day. Once you start this challenge, however, if you entertain one unkind thought about that person, you are to replace it with not just one but ten kind thoughts, ten good qualities not on that list. This forces you to keep looking for good qualities."

I made the conscious decision to reject all of the negative thoughts about Jerry I had looked for before. I realized, of course, this exercise was never to be used as a form of denial or an excuse to avoid conflict. I just wanted to break my bad habit of looking for the worst in my hard-working and loyal husband.

By daily reminding myself of 2 Corinthians 10:5 about holding every thought captive and bringing it into obedience to Christ, I was able to go two entire weeks without letting one negative thought about my husband get a foothold in my mind. I was ecstatic!

The very next day, however, I suffered a major setback and discovered a brutal truth—it would take me longer than 30 days to accomplish my goal. The rule was that whenever you allowed one negative thought about that person to dwell in your mind, you failed and had to start over again, from day one. Yikes!

"Lord, at this rate it's going to be a lifelong task for me!" I complained.

Bingo! His spirit whispered into my soul.

With God's help, I finally made my goal. Thirty wonderful consecutive days free of negative thoughts about my husband! What amazed me more than that unbelievable accomplishment, however, was how much my husband had improved in that short period of time!

I realized later, that all of Jerry's many good qualities, now embedded in my mind, were reflected in my speech and actions toward him—which stirred new love in his heart for me. Even more importantly, I had developed a lifelong practice that became the norm rather than the exception.

God not only restored my lost love for Jerry, but He replaced it with an even deeper love. This love enveloped us both, and grew stronger until we admitted, many years later, that we were more in love then than even in the beginning. We rarely went to sleep without holding hands and saying, "I love you."

Our love lasted until he went home to heaven, after 47 years of marriage. All because God answered my fervent prayer one stormy night, "Help me to love my husband."

"PLEASE HELP MY HORSE!"

Marilyn Morris Mayer

Slick was my dream horse. A five-year-old sorrel quarter horse, he was always up for a ride on the trails or a weekend at the horse shows.

One August, I took him with me all the way from Kansas City, Missouri, to South Fork, Colorado, to participate in a weeklong training session on new, gentler methods of teaching horses. I joined twenty other horse owners in a spartan inn the man teaching the sessions, John, had leased near an abandoned ranch. We were pretty much alone out there but for the smoke coming from the cabins higher up in the Rockies.

Having hauled from east of Colorado, I put aside thoughts of my arduous journey through La Veta Pass, a windswept mountain road between Pueblo and South Fork, to enjoy the fresh mountain air and the horses.

We got up at six o'clock each morning to drive to the barns and feed our horses. We cleaned their feet and brushed their coats before heading back to a hearty breakfast prepared by the woman who owned the inn. Then we were off again to the ranch for hours of riding and training under a canopy of sunshine that made Slick's coppery-red coat sparkle like gold.

I could see that he was enjoying new equine friends to visit with and, of course, the extra hay to munch on during the "class-room" breaks from the work.

On the next-to-last night there, we rode up into the wooded hills and had a cookout. While our horses enjoyed their grain, some of us gathered around the campfire with our hot dogs and potato chips and started telling "That's nothin'!" stories about our riding misadventures. Someone told how a branch caught her on the chin and knocked her right off her mount and into a mud puddle.

"That's nothing!" said John's wife, Susie. "Once, I took my horse to a hydrant for a drink. Only I accidentally got his halter caught on the pump handle. I couldn't get him free. He began to panic, and I knew we were in trouble. Finally I just stopped and prayed. And the next try, I got him free."

"But I thought prayer was only for the really big things, like when someone you loved was gravely ill," I said.

"No," Susie said. "I pray anytime I need help. God doesn't mind helping with big problems or small ones."

John joined us at the campfire. "It's getting dark," he said. "Guess we'd better be heading back."

We climbed on our horses and picked along the rocky trail back to the barn, chatting as we rode. It was nearly midnight by the time we'd put our horses in their dark stalls and given them an extra ration of hay. We headed back to the inn, exhausted.

The next morning, I cleaned the dirt and rocks from Slick's feet. I noticed he wasn't putting his weight on his right front foot and it was really swollen. It was hot to the touch. I was sure I was looking at a bowed tendon, a serious injury that can happen when a horse's legs are under too much physical stress.

Guilt welled up within me, seeing the pain in Slick's eyes. Why hadn't I checked him over more carefully before heading back to the inn the night before? Had the trail ride been too much after the day's training session? I'd come all this way to find gentler ways to train Slick. Now he might end up permanently lame. Every moment was precious. I needed to ice the leg to halt any further damage, then get the help of a veterinarian.

I rushed to John and asked about a vet, but he didn't know of any in the area. All of us—including John—were strangers to these parts.

"I have an ice boot you can use," John said. "You run back to the inn and get some ice. We'll figure out something after that."

I drove my truck down the mountain road at breakneck speed, my thoughts racing about as fast. I didn't just need a veterinarian—I needed a horse specialist. And they are usually found only in heavily populated areas. Would there be one in Pueblo? Or would I need to haul Slick 210 miles to Colorado Springs to one of the large vet clinics?

Either way, that meant driving through treacherous La Veta Pass. It was scary enough hauling on that mountain road with a horse balancing on four good feet. If he were to lose his balance and collapse because of the injury, it could send us hurtling over the steep cliff. And all that was if—if the horse could even be loaded in the trailer. It was painful for him just to move.

Susie's words came back to me now. *God doesn't mind helping us with anything, big or small.* "Please, God, please help my horse,"

I prayed aloud, repeating the words over and over until I reached the inn. I ran inside to the kitchen and filled a plastic bag with as much ice as I could carry.

"What happened?" the innkeeper asked. I gave a quick explanation and asked if she knew any veterinarians in the area. "No, I'm sorry," she replied. I hurried to the front door.

"I'll say a prayer for your horse," the innkeeper said. It was beginning to seem like this praying for anything wasn't as unusual as I had thought. With a quick "Thank you" I headed out the inn's door.

What I saw next stopped me in my tracks. A white truck was pulling into the drive. In a flash I saw the symbol on the side—a medical staff and snake with a large V in the middle. An equine veterinarian's truck! Could it be possible?

I ran to the truck driver. "Are you a veterinarian?" I asked. With a good-natured smile he assured me he was.

"My horse is hurt. His leg is all swollen. I'm afraid he's bowed a tendon. He's about ten miles away in the mountains," I continued. "Is there any way you could come look at him today?"

"I'll come right now. Lead the way."

As we sped back up the mountain road, I watched my rearview mirror to make sure I didn't lose him. I also had to keep reminding myself he was real. At last we reached the ranch.

"Hello there, Fellow. Let me take a look and see what we have here." The vet knelt down to feel Slick's leg.

"We were riding late last night, then this morning I found him like this."

"Did you clean his feet already this morning?" the vet asked.

"Yes," I said.

"Did he have a rock in this foot?"

I nodded. The vet stood up and patted Slick on the neck.

"Your horse doesn't have a bowed tendon. I believe he picked up a rock during your ride, and held his foot in a cramped position overnight. That's what caused the swelling." He wrapped the leg and explained that I should keep icing it throughout the day. "He'll be able to travel tomorrow," he assured me, as tears welled up in my eyes.

"Thanks," I said. I gave Slick a big hug.

"What do I owe you?" I asked.

The veterinarian loaded his things and got back in his truck. "Nothing," he said, flashing that good-natured smile. "I'm not working today. I just took the day off from my practice in Colorado Springs to do some fishing out here."

I was glad he'd picked that day to drive more than two hundred miles, right to where he was needed. Now I knew, firsthand, what Susie had told us about praying for whatever you need.

"You take care of that horse now," the vet called from his window when he passed me going back down the road. As he drove away, I swear the veterinarian symbol on his truck looked just like angel's wings.

ABLAZE!

John J. Wright

I stared up at the forty stories of pipes, girders, and cranes topped by an orange exhaust flame shooting high in the sky, so bright it seemed to dim the moon.

I was standing on the world's largest semi-submersible oilrig. In thirty years since I'd started my own manufacturing company, I'd never before seen such an incredible example of technology in all its glory. There, eighty miles off the coast of Brazil, with the din of machinery and workers all around, I felt an overwhelming sense of awe at man's ingenuity.

I had come there that March day last year with two of my staff members, William Brombeck and Robert Lamont, to supervise the installation of our company's replacement electrohydraulic actuators for the rig's ballast. These would help raise and lower the rig.

We were a long way from home back in New York but that was nothing new. I'd built my business by being hands-on. I liked to see the equipment in action, supervise the fine-tuning myself. People were always asking me when I would retire. But at 75 I couldn't think of anything else I'd rather be doing. Except for my diabetes, which I could control with medication, God had kept me in good health, and I wanted to put my abilities to good use. Hard work was my way of thanking Him for His blessings.

One of those many blessings was my family. Kathleen and I had been married for fifty years. Our five children had long since flown the coop and had kids of their own, but they all lived nearby. Almost all of them had gone into medicine. I marveled at the way they could heal an injured body just as I did at the way the men on this rig could draw oil from beneath the ocean floor.

The rig had been a sight to behold from the helicopter we'd flown in on that morning—the length of three football fields, like a giant steel beast lying on the sea. There were 175 men hard at work drilling for oil, sending some to a hulking tanker behind us for processing.

The rig's designers seemed to have thought of everything, from state-of-the-art drilling machinery to exhaustive safety measures, including powerful fireboats. The officers even made sure that the insulin I needed for my diabetes was carefully stored for safekeeping in the infirmary's refrigerator.

Still, most impressive of all was that towering orange exhaust flare. I took a photograph of it before I headed to my stateroom.

I got settled and went to sleep at about 10:00 PM. We were set to begin replacing the rig's defective actuators with our company's new ones early the next morning.

A loud jangling noise jolted me wide awake. I glanced at the clock. 12:15 AM. Had to be a fire drill. I wondered if they weren't taking this safety thing just a little too far. Couldn't they schedule a drill at a decent hour?

I pulled on my robe and slippers and grudgingly grabbed my life jacket. In the passageway a safety officer rushed toward me. "Mr. Wright, go back and get dressed and put shoes on!" he said.

What's going on? I wondered. I'd been through hundreds of these drills and had never had to put shoes on! Quickly pulling on my clothes and shoes, I left my stateroom. I headed toward the infirmary to get my insulin—just in case.

Suddenly a tremendous explosion shook the rig, like a roar from the bottom of the ocean itself. I grabbed a rail to keep from falling. There were yells, people running in every direction.

Two officers ran past me carrying a man between them, the top half of his uniform burned off. My mind was flooded with questions. What had caused the explosion? Was there a fire? Where were Brombeck and Lamont?

I glanced up at the orange exhaust flare spiking into the blackness. Now it didn't seem so bright and powerful. Suddenly I felt how alone we were, so many miles from the mainland, floating on waters 4,300 feet deep.

Slowly, steadily, I made my way through the confusion toward the fluorescent lights of the infirmary. I backed against the wall as horribly burned men were rushed in on stretchers, their clothes in charred tatters. I learned an oil leak had sparked a fire in the support columns.

In a moment I had retrieved my insulin from the refrigerator. But what about these poor young guys all around me? If only I had my children's medical knowledge! If only I could do something to help.

From outside came another thunderous explosion. The room convulsed, glass bottles falling from shelves and shattering on the floor. I braced myself against the wall. Someone rushed in and yelled, "Everyone prepare to evacuate!"

I went back out on deck. The flare had been turned off but now I saw flames almost as bright at the other end of the rig. The fireboats spewed seawater at the blaze. Off to the side, cranes clanked, lowering men down into workboats, four at a time.

It was like something out of a disaster movie. The flames played across the boats so that now you saw them, and now you didn't. The rig was already listing badly. The flames shot up for a moment and illuminated the right pontoon. It was covered with water. The pontoons couldn't be raised because of the broken actuators. *We're going to sink!* It didn't seem possible, not this mammoth creation with its mazes of iron, its levers and pulleys and meters and valves—but the rig was going under.

The deck lurched and tilted farther. I had to lean to one side to keep my balance. The fire still danced savagely in the darkness. Lights blinked on and off as the gas turbines on the rig cut in and out. I had a sudden image of another of man's great technological wonders—the Titanic—sinking into a deep-sea grave.

It was about one-thirty. About 25 of us were still left on the rig. The captain called us together. "Everyone on the other deck has been transferred to the tanker behind us," he announced. "The rest of us will be off of here soon."

The captain came to my side and assured me Brombeck and Lamont were safe. "There's a copter coming from Rio at three. You'll be on it."

I thanked him but I couldn't help wondering how the chopper would land on the severely angled rig.

I looked down at the insulin in my hand. The children had

been so worried when I got diabetes, afraid I wouldn't slow down enough to look after my health. Yet I'd always been careful about taking my twice-daily shot.

I was fortunate I'd been able to get my insulin, but I was still racing against time. I could barely keep my feet as the rig swayed amid the pounding waves. Men gripped the railings, quiet and grim. I felt as helpless now as I had felt confident when I first set foot on the rig just that morning.

I looked up to where the flare had been, wishing it were still there. But then I realized it was useless. It couldn't be seen by my family in New York. It couldn't make the helicopter pilot arrive any faster to rescue us. It couldn't stop the relentless waves from washing over the pontoons, slowly pulling us into the depths.

I closed my eyes. *God, please let me see my family again. My wife and children and grandchildren. Only You can help us.*

It didn't matter how remote we were, how dark it was, how dire the situation—God could still see us and hear us and be with us out here on this rig. Where technology's power ran out, His began. Where man's strength fails, His never falters. Over and over I asked God to see us through, even as more explosions wracked the crippled rig.

I heard the whir of a copter. We cheered. The pilot tried to lower the craft. The landing pad had tilted to a thirty-degree angle. Lord, guide him, I prayed. We stood silently, watching. The chopper finally, tentatively, set down on the lopsided pad, its rotors still spinning loudly to keep it steady.

We dashed to the helipad. Another explosion sounded above us. Falling metal clanged so loudly it felt like the sound was coming from inside my head. A large pipe landed just a few feet away.

"Come on!" someone said, and we rushed to the helipad.

I watched two medics carrying a stretcher up to the copter. On it lay a burn victim moaning softly. I was overwhelmed by powerlessness.

Dear God, please give that man strength, I prayed. *Give all the injured strength. Help them.*

I felt stronger after praying. Amid all that madness, clinging to the tilting deck, the fire raging wildly, the roar of the copter filling my ears, the thing I sensed most acutely was God's presence and power when I reached out to Him in prayer.

I pulled myself into the helicopter and hunched down. In moments the door was shut and the copter strained up into the air—only to drop toward the ocean.

White foam leapt up out of the darkness. Time stretched out like an oil slick as we hung between sky and sea, life and death.

Finally the copter gained enough momentum, and we flew away from the raging flames and the great steel beast groaning in the darkness. We were safe.

Two days later I was back in New York, tired but unbelievably grateful to see my family again. The following Monday I was back running my company, Brombeck and Lamont at my side.

These days I'm still awed by the complex machines men build and the technology that makes them work—but I know now that the workings of prayer are the most mysterious and powerful of all. And that my greatest strength comes from my faith, one flame that will always burn bright.

BUDGET LIVING

Monica McGill

I looked at my gift list. I couldn't possibly afford presents for all the friends and family. How had it gotten so out of control?

Lord, Christmas is getting too expensive. Help me think of budget-friendly gifts.

Some families do Secret Santas, where one person gets the name of one other person, and that's it. Good for the pocketbook, but it seemed to me there had to be a way to give something to all the people I loved.

I talked it over with my husband and our kids. What was the one thing we could afford to give everyone? Our time! But how?

Then it came to me: prayer. I'd turn my gift list into a weekly prayer list. Each person would get his or her own week.

I went out to the store and bought a calendar and filled the months with names. Then the kids hand-drew a little flyer, which I made copies of.

We personalized each with a name. Next to each name was that person's week, so they would know exactly when prayers were going up on their behalf.

The flyers got sent out along with our Christmas cards. I have to admit, I felt a bit sheepish about the whole thing. I couldn't help wondering, *Will they think we're cheapskates? Worse, will they think we are nuts?*

Right after Christmas I started getting phone calls and e-mails. "How did you know I needed praying for?" one dear friend asked.

"What a sweet idea," said another grateful caller. "How on earth did you ever come up with it?"

How could I explain that prayer was the answer to prayer?

These days, people on our list send prayer requests right before their week. It's become a family tradition, and budget-friendly, too.

LEARNING *to* LISTEN

Whitney Von Lake Hopler

A monitor beeped to signal that my mom's blood transfusion was complete, and I glanced up to see that the clear bag on the IV pole above her hospital bed was empty.

"I'll get a nurse," I said, starting to rise from my chair.

"Oh, don't worry about that," Mom replied as she adjusted the cap that covered her bald head. "Someone will be in soon." She smiled and reached over to the nightstand beside her bed to retrieve a box of chocolate candy. "Want one?"

"Okay. Thanks."

As I bit into the creamy chocolate, I tried to focus on its sweet scent and ignore the overpowering aroma of disinfectant in the room.

"So . . . " Mom began, but her voice trailed off for a moment as a rare serious expression crossed her face.

A long pause sat between us like an uninvited guest. Was Mom finally willing to talk about faith? Even after being diagnosed with terminal leukemia, she'd change the subject when I tried to ask about her relationship with God.

She'd been this way for more than twenty years. I'd tried to talk to her about spiritual things. I wanted her to find salvation; she wanted me to "lighten up." Now Mom seemed lost in thought so I leaned in closer.

"You know what, Mom?" I said eagerly. "God knows what you're going through, and He cares. He sent Jesus—"

"So what has Honor been up to at school?" Mom interrupted with a nervous smile, asking about my eight-year-old.

"Um, well, she's working on a project about geography where she has to invent a pretend country and design a map of it," I replied, talking fast. "But as I was saying about God . . . ."

"Oh, there's the nurse now," Mom said as she spotted a nurse approaching from the hallway. Mom gestured toward the chocolate box. "Here, Dear, why don't you have another one while she takes down the bag?"

I just sighed and reached for another chocolate. As the nurse worked, I stared at the plastic IV tubes entering Mom's body and wished I could order her a faith transfusion as easily as her doctors could order a blood transfusion. No matter how hard I'd tried over the years, my efforts to bring Mom to faith had failed—and sometimes even backfired.

Once, on a trip we took to Europe, I'd been too zealous about asking her to pray with me inside St. Peter's Basilica at the Vatican. She countered that she was just there to see the artwork, and nothing was wrong with that. After I argued that no one should visit a cathedral without praying inside, she refused to even step inside the massive church at all.

After that I tried to be more aware of when our discussions about spiritual issues became less like conversations and more like lectures. I started to talk less to Mom about God, and began to talk more to God about Mom.

Then, gradually, Mom abandoned her agnostic stance and told me she believed that God exists. Unfortunately, she wasn't ready to begin a relationship with Him. She went as far as coming to church with me on special occasions like Christmas, and would sometimes let me pray for her about a current challenge in her life. But she always added, "Be sure to make it short."

If I rambled too long, she'd just cut me off with an "Amen" and a smile that combined affection and amusement.

Just after she'd finally expressed some interest in going to church more frequently, she met a man through an Internet dating service, and impulsively moved in with him in Nevada. My concerns about her living with him closed off all of our spiritual conversations for a while after that.

Not until she'd left her boyfriend and moved back to Virginia several years later did she again seem open to talking about God and visiting church. A few months later, she was diagnosed with acute myelogenous leukemia and landed in a local hospital for nearly two months of grueling chemotherapy. Doctors didn't expect her to go into remission, but Mom was willing to do whatever it took to try to gain some more time.

The nurse finished taking down the blood transfusion bag and left the room. I glanced at the clock on the wall; I had to go soon in order to pick Honor up from school on time.

"Well, Mom, I'll stop by your apartment later to pick up your mail," I said, rising from my chair to give her a good-bye hug and kiss. "and I'll be sure to bring that in with me when I come to visit tomorrow morning."

"Okay. Thanks, Whitney," Mom replied, the serious expression crossing her face once more. "And," she paused, pondering something in her mind, then finally spoke in a near-whisper. "And I haven't told you the most important thing."

"What's that?"

"I saw an angel," Mom blurted out. Then she searched my face carefully to see how I would react.

"An angel?" I sank back down into my chair. It wouldn't hurt to be a few minutes late picking up Honor.

"Really," Mom said, with awe in her voice. "I know it must sound crazy, but it really happened."

"I believe you," I assured her. "Angels are real."

"Yes—yes they are." Mom's face lit up with excitement as she told me the story. "It was last night. I was sitting in a chair by the window there while two nurses were changing my bed. And when I first saw the angel across the courtyard, I turned away and thought, *I can't really be seeing what I think I'm seeing.* But when I looked again, she was still there, looking straight at me."

"Were you afraid?"

"No, that's the funny thing. I felt more peace than I've ever felt before." Mom reached for my hand and squeezed it. "And she was so beautiful. She was lit from within with a very powerful light that didn't hurt my eyes. And those wings! Such intricate designs, like ripples of white, cream, and chestnut brown that matched her brown hair." Mom paused to let me speak, but I decided to do something wiser instead: listen.

"The angel raised her hands and gestured to me like this," Mom said, moving her hands gracefully in a circular sweeping motion. "And then she sent me something."

"What was it?"

Mom shook her head. "I have no idea. But there were about four or five of them. They looked like oval-shaped bits of energy. The outlines of the ovals were like glowing gold, and the insides were transparent. They came out of the angel's hands, across the courtyard, through the window, and into my chest."

Mom studied my face again as if she was afraid I might laugh at her.

But I leaned in closer and embraced her instead. "Did you feel anything when that happened?"

"No, nothing physically. But now . . . . " Mom searched for the right words. "It was all so overwhelming! I wasn't ever religious before. But now, I'm a true believer!"

Lung scan results showed that the angel's mysterious bits of energy had apparently cleared up severe pneumonia in Mom's lungs. And a bone marrow test revealed another gift—Mom had gone into remission, much to her doctors' surprise. But the greatest gift of all was the change in Mom's soul.

After God showed Mom that He loved her so much He was even willing to send one of His heavenly messengers her way, Mom began to seek Him in earnest.

And for the rest of the time she had left to live—until she passed away two months later from an infection—she initiated the conversations about God. I didn't have to ask her permission to pray with her anymore, because she was eager to pray, and even those long prayers were fine. Through the angel He'd sent, God blessed Mom with just enough time to place her trust in Him.

Shortly before she died, Mom had gotten up the courage to

tell the story of her angelic encounter to a few people, like my sister, Courtney, a nurse at the hospital, a hospital chaplain, and a pastor from our church. And she let me interview her so I could keep telling her story after she was gone. I sat in silence, scribbling down notes, knowing that the best gift I could give Mom wasn't talking—it was simply listening.

AUTHOR BIOGRAPHIES

Yulia Bagwell was born in Ukraine. She received her B.A. degree in Belarus and Masters in America. Now she and her husband, Jesse, live in Philadelphia.

Tonya Brown is a product of the Midwest, transported to a North Carolina beach. Her career paths include teacher, librarian, mentoring coordinator, and freelance writer.

Pamela J. Caldwell is in the Communications Department at Cal State Fullerton and is senior editor of *Precious Times Magazine*. A mother of two and grandmother of eight, she also oversees the outreach team at Beacon Church.

Marvel Castro lives in Syracuse, New York.

Kitty Chappell, an award-winning author of two books, *Sins of a Father* and *Good Mews, Inspurrrational Stories for Cat Lovers,* lives with her cat, Miss Middy, in Chandler, Arizona. www.kittychappell.com.

Stephen Clover has had two children's books published. In 2009 he won first prize in the Invercargill Writers Sandwich Competition. He holds diplomas in freelance journalism and children's writing, and writes from his home in New Zealand.

Shirley Corder is a freelance writer, registered nurse, and pastor's wife. She lives in South Africa, and writes inspirational stories and articles. Visit her website at www.shirleycorder.com.

Betty J. Dalrymple is a contributor to many devotional books. She facilitates a grief-support group, enjoys playing golf, traveling, and spending time with her new husband and their large blended family.

Genell Dawson was living in Rancho Santa Margarita, California, when she experienced this touch of God's answered prayer.

Midge DeSart and her husband, Keith, have been married for 45 years. Midge is the author of *Maintaining Balance In A Stress-Filled World.*

William H. Eastburn has made Buckingham, Pennsylvania, his home.

Shawnelle Eliason is a 2008 Guideposts Writers Workshop winner. She's been published in *Guideposts, Hearts at Home* magazine, *Momsense,* and *Christmas Miracles.*

Paul D. Grams writes from Rockford, Illinois.

Thomas J. Haggai is the IGA Global president, chairman and CEO, and non-executive chairman of IGA, INC.

Bob Haslam has served as pastor, missionary, editor of *Light and Life* magazine, and has been published in more than 75 publications and eight books. He mentors 51 budding writers.

Whitney Von Lake Hopler has authored hundreds of articles and several books. As an editor, she's served at The Salvation Army's national magazines, Crosswalk.com, and several newspapers..

Ronnie J. Johnson, Ph.D., is a professor at BMA Theological Seminary in Jacksonville, Texas. He is author of *Cows, Pigs, and Chickens Made Me a Better Teacher.* www.RonnieJohnson.info.

Eva Juliuson once heard someone say, "If you're going to the throne room of God, then grab someone's hand and take him or her with you!" That's what she's been doing ever since! She sends out short e-mail prayers to inspire others to pray about anything and everything! To receive these prayers, contact evajuliuson@hotmail.com.

Ron Lantz is at home in Ludlow, Kentucky.

Kevin Lucia writes from his home in Castle Creek, New York.

Christy Ogden Marsh is from Wrightsville Beach, North Carolina.

Marilyn Morris Mayer combines her love for horses and her love for writing from her home in Kansas City, Missouri.

Monica McGill is from Cape Coral, Florida.

Guillerma Merancio is from Tucson, Arizona, and her story is told by Lupe Ruiz-Flores.

Mary Kay Moody writes short stories, articles, and a suspense series. She works to prevent violence, and assist trauma victims. She also helps others by leading a domestic violence ministry at her church. www.MaryKayMoody.com..

Jim Ness is from Wasilla, Alaska.

Nairy Ohanian has served as a campus minister and missionary in the United States and abroad. She lived ten years in Armenia and Turkey. She loves to tell stories and is working on a doctoral program in Pastoral Counseling for Missionaries.

Betty Ost-Everley is married to Terry, and mother to two. Besides writing, Betty is also a neighborhood activist, serving Christ by serving the people in her area.

Donald E. Phillips is a former chaplain, professor, and pastor. He has authored four internationally-recognized academic books, as well as shorter writings.

Connie K. Pombo is is an author, speaker, freelance writer, and founder of Women's Mentoring Ministries in Mt. Joy, Pennsylvania. She is the contributing author to several anthologies. www.conniepombo.com.

Kelly Ruffcorn lives in Spokane, Washington, with her husband and two daughters. She has a degree in English and elementary education and is a freelance writer.

Julie Saffrin writes fiction and nonfiction and enjoys freelance projects. She has had more than one hundred articles and essays published. She loves big water and lappy waves. www.juliesaffrin.com.

Katherine Valentine is author of the highly praised Dorsetville novels (Penguin/Doubleday) and a speaker who has appeared on Biography Channel's mini-series, *The Apostles, Lifetime,* and *Good Morning America.* www.katherinevalentine.com.

Wayne Vanderpoel is from Pinellas Park, Florida.

Stacy Voss continues to be convicted of the power of prayer by her daughter, son, and husband. She lives in the Denver area and is a co-founder and contributor of www.meetmeattheintersection.com.

Wallace Wanlund learned his lessons in prayer from San Pedro, California.

Susan M. Watkins is an award-winning author and scriptwriter, who formerly wrote for "The 700 Club." She's written for several devotional books, *Atlanta-Journal Constitution,* and various professional newsletters.

Ted Weaver is a writer, public speaker, and educator. Ministry to prisoners and the homeless, woodworking, and writing fill his Colorado life.

Rose Renee Wirth, wife, mother, and grandmother, has been included in several compilations. Her subjects range from hormones to healing from sexual abuse.

John J. Wright is right at home not only on big rigs, but also is right at home in New York.

WHEN YOU NEED TO PRAY FOR...

A NOTE FROM THE EDITORS

Guideposts, a nonprofit organization, touches millions of lives every day through products and services that inspire, encourage and uplift. Our magazines, books, prayer network and outreach programs help people connect their faith-filled values to their daily lives. To learn more, visit www.guideposts.com or www.guidepostsfoundation.org.

The Extraordinary Answers to Prayer series has been created by Guideposts to affirm readers everywhere in the extraordinary ways prayer makes a difference in all our lives. If you have a personal prayer request, write to our volunteers at Guideposts Prayer Fellowship, PO Box 5813, Harlan, IA 51593-1313, call (845) 704-6080, or visit our website at OurPrayer.org to post your request, find additional resources, or to join our online prayer community.